NATIONS of the WORLD

SAMUEL BRIMSON

Library of Congress Cataloging-in-Publication Data available
upon request from publisher. Fax (414) 336-0157 for the attention
of the Publishing Records Department.

ISBN 0-8368-5489-6

This North American edition first published in 2004 by
World Almanac® Library,
330 West Olive Street, Suite 100, Milwaukee, WI 53212 USA.

Created by Trocadero Publishing, an Electra Media Group
Enterprise, Suite 204, 74 Pitt Street, Sydney NSW 2000, Australia.

Original copyright © 2003 S. and L. Brodie.

WORLD ALMANAC® LIBRARY

North Korea

DEMOCRATIC PEOPLE'S REPUBLIC OF KOREA

North Korea is part of a peninsula in northeastern Asia. A series of ranges runs from the northeast to the southwest, separated by deep, narrow valleys with short, unnavigable rivers. The western side of the peninsula features wide coastal plains. The climate varies a good deal. Summers can be extremely hot. The Siberian air mass often brings severe cold and snow in the winters.

The people of North Korea are nearly all of a Korean background. Officially, there is no religion as it is considered contrary to communist ideology. The indigenous Ch'ondogyo, which combines elements of Buddhism, Confucianism, and Christianity, is practiced in private by some people. The official language is Korean.

Low levels of fertility and bad land management have meant North Korea has had limited success with farming. The country is in dire condition at present, with widespread malnutrition and starvation because of crop failures. As many as one million people died during the 1990s.

Mining is important to the North Korean economy. There are significant deposits of iron ore, coal, gold, tungsten and graphite. The coal and iron ore mining industries have been substantially upgraded in recent years to increase export potential. There are also large reserves of uranium, silver, lead, copper, zinc and manganese. North Korea's principal manufactured items include military equipment, machinery, refined metals and textiles.

The North Korean government was led by the president from 1972 until 1998. The head of state is now the chairman of the National Defense Commission. The Supreme People's

North Korea viewed across the demilitarized zone at Panmunjom.

FLAT EARTH PICTURE GALLERY

Assembly, whose members are elected for a four-year term, gives a superficial impression of democracy.

The earliest known Korean state was Old Choson, in what is now western North Korea and Manchuria. Chinese forces conquered it in about 100 B.C. The Chinese later coexisted with the native kingdom of Koguryo. Two additional native kingdoms, Paekche and Silla, were founded in the south in the 3rd century A.D.

Each of the kingdoms rose to a position of strength. The three kingdoms were in conflict with one another for centuries. Silla allied with China in the late seventh century to conquer Koguryo and Paekche.

This period was known as the United Silla. It saw relative peace and a flowering of artistic activities. Buddhism was the state religion. Confucianism provided the pattern for government and daily life.

Wang Kon peacefully ended the United Silla era in 935 to found his own Koryo dynasty. Everything progressed peacefully until 1231, when invading Mongol armies began a thirty-year war. The resulting Mongol–Koryo alliance lasted until 1392. A new social and political reform inspired the founding of the Choson dynasty, under Yi Songgye.

The Choson dynasty lasted just over 600 years. It was based at Seoul. The government's political structure was based on Confucianism. A phonetic alphabet was developed and printing presses were invented.

Japan invaded in 1592, beginning a six-year conflict that brought incredible destruction and bloodshed. Korea eventually triumphed with the aid of China's Ming dynasty. Multiple invasions by the Chinese Manchu followed. This forced the Choson to build its own strength beyond Chinese influence.

The Choson dynasty enjoyed capable leadership and economic growth during the next two centuries. Christianity was introduced in 1784. It was later outlawed under King Taewongun in 1864. Japan forced the Choson dynasty to sign a trade treaty in 1876. Korea did not want to be locked into a relationship with Japan alone, so it signed other trade agreements with European nations and the United States.

Korea was forced to let Japanese troops use it as a route into Manchuria when Japan went to war with Russia in 1904. Japan unexpectedly defeated Russia, but kept its troops in place. The peninsula was annexed by Japan in 1910, ending the Choson dynasty.

Korea both suffered and benefited under Japanese control. A network of railways was

GOVERNMENT
Capital Pyongyang
Type of government
Communist dictatorship
Independence from Japan
August 15, 1945
Voting Universal adult suffrage
Head of state Chairman of the National Defence Committee
Head of government Premier
Constitution 1948, 1972
Legislature
Unicameral Supreme People's Assembly
Judiciary Central Court
Member of UN, UNESCO, WHO

LAND AND PEOPLE
Land area 46,540 sq mi
(120,538 sq km)
Highest point My. Paektu
9,003 ft (2,744 m)
Coastline 1,550 mi (2,495 km)
Population 22,224,195
Major cities and populations
Pyongyang 2,250,000
Hamhung 700,000
Chongjin 550,000
Ethnic groups
Korean 99%, Chinese 1%
Religions officially discouraged
Languages Korean

ECONOMIC
Currency North Korean won
Industry
armaments, machinery, chemicals; mining, metallurgy, textiles, food processing
Agriculture
rice, corn, potatoes, soybeans, pulses, cattle, pigs
Natural resources
coal, lead, tungsten, zinc, graphite, magnesite, iron ore, copper, gold, pyrites, salt, fluorspar

North Korea

built, communications upgraded, modern factories constructed and exploitation of rich mineral deposits began. Liberation groups worked to expel the Japanese, but they were weak and disorganized. Millions of Koreans took part in a peaceful demonstration in 1919. This was called the March First Movement. The expected foreign support did not come and the Japanese merely tightened their hold.

The Allied forces began planning for the withdrawal of Japanese troops prior to the end of World War II. The United Nations divided Korea into two zones of occupation at the 38th parallel. Soviet troops occupied the north, Americans the south. Each worked to gain cooperation from citizens while dealing with the removal of the Japanese. Koreans hoped for unification. The U.S. and the Soviet Union began arranging separate governments in 1947.

The Soviet Union vetoed all U.N. moves for reunification and free elections. All trade and travel between the two zones ceased as Cold War tensions grew. The Korean economy was in chaos. The north had the industries and mineral resources, while the south had the agriculture. Desperate Koreans tried to escape communism by fleeing south.

Two separate states, the Democratic People's Republic of Korea (North Korea) and the Republic of Korea (South Korea) were established in 1948. Kim Il Sung emerged as leader of North Korea. All foreign troops were withdrawn from both countries during 1949. The Soviet Union ensured North Korea had its own large, well-equipped army, unlike the South.

North Korean troops crossed the 38th parallel into the South on June 25, 1950. United States President Harry Truman mobilized U.S. forces. The United Nations assembled an multinational coalition to defend South Korea, commanded by General Douglas MacArthur.

The North Koreans encountered little resistance from the South Korean army and a small U.S. force. The North Koreans had pushed their opponents into an area around Pusan by September 10, 1950. On September 15, 1950 MacArthur staged a highly successful landing at Inchon. The invaders began withdrawing. They returned to North Korea by September 27th.

The United Nations forces pursued them into the North. They had reached the Yalu River, the border between Korea and China, by late November. A vast Chinese army stormed into North Korea, scattering the United Nations forces. The communists had taken Seoul, the capital of South Korea by January of 1951.

The United Nations tried to negotiate a cease-fire through peace talks. Fighting continued because the Soviets would not agree to the U. N. terms for the peaceful exchange of prisoners. A truce was finally signed on July 27, 1953. Neither side gained any new territory.

North Korea began an ambitious program of industrialization. Soviet Union financial aid enabled the construction of railways and the modernization of industrial plants. All industries were nationalized. Agriculture was managed under a government collective. The people of the nation became very harshly controlled.

Reunification talks began again in 1972 and continued through the 1980s. North Korea remains a closed society. Tourism is strictly limited. All media is state controlled.

When Kim Il Sung died in 1994, control passed to his son, Kim Jong Il. A summit took place between Kim Dae Jung of South Korea and Kim Jong Il of North Korea to discuss reunification. U. S. President George W. Bush expressed concern over North Korea's continued build-up of nuclear weapons. North Korea withdrew from the Nuclear Non-Proliferation Treaty and reactivated its main nuclear plant in early 2003.

South Korea

REPUBLIC OF KOREA

Occupying the southern part of the Korean Peninsula in eastern Asia, South Korea is bordered on the north by North Korea and on all other sides by bodies of water. It also includes more than 3400 islands to the south and west. A series of mountains runs down the eastern coast, the principal being the Taebaek-sanmaek Range. They are separated by deep, narrow valleys through which often run short, unnavigable rivers. The western and southern sides of the peninsula feature wide coastal plains.

Although South Korea's climate is classified as temperate, its geography produces some unusual effects. Air masses from Siberia produce severe winter cold and snow, particularly in the mountains of the north.

Almost everyone in South Korea is of Korean heritage. Christianity is the dominant faith. Buddhism is also very strong. Chondogyo, a combination of aspects of the Buddhist, Confucian and Tao faiths, has a strong presence as well. The official language is Korean.

Only about twenty percent of the land in South Korea is suitable for agriculture. Half of that is devoted to rice cultivation. The seas around the Korean peninsula have abundant seafood. Korean fishers sail great distances for their catch, even into the southern hemisphere.

South Korea experienced a period of economic instability and shaky governments after the end of the Korean War in 1953. The nation has focused on industrial development since the 1961 *coup d'état* which brought General Park Chung Hee to power.

South Korea has become a major exporter of manufactured goods in recent decades. Its main exports once included only clothing, textiles and processed foods. The nation's heavy industries now produce motor vehicles, ships, steel, chemicals as well as electronic equipment and components.

FLAT EARTH PICTURE GALLERY

South Korea

FLAT EARTH PICTURE GALLERY

Climbers in the Sorak San National Park.

South Korea is a democratic republic. Its original constitution of 1948 has been amended several times. The president, elected by the people for five years, appoints the prime minister and cabinet. Members of the unicameral National Assembly are also elected by popular vote for a four-year term.

The earliest known Korean state was Old Choson, in what is now western North Korea and Manchuria. The Chinese conquered Old Choson in about 108 B.C. China founded colonies in Korea while the native kingdom of Koguryo began to grow. Two additional kingdoms, Paekche and Silla, emerged in the south in the third and fourth centuries A.D. Each of the three kingdoms Koguryo, Paekche and Silla —

sought to dominate the others. Silla allied with China to conquer Koguryo and Paekche in the seventh century.

The following period, known as the United Silla, saw relative peace and a flowering of artistic activities. Buddhism had grown to become the dominant faith of Korea. Confucianism became the pattern for government and daily life.

Wang Kon ended the Silla era in 935 to found his own Koryo dynasty. The people of the kingdom lived in relative peace for about three centuries. Mongol armies invaded in 1231, beginning a thirty-year war. The resulting Mongol–Koryo alliance lasted until 1392. A new social and political reform movement inspired the founding of the Choson dynasty, under Yi Songgye.

The Choson dynasty lasted just over 600 years with its capital at Seoul. Its political structure was based on Confucianism. A phonetic alphabet was developed and printing presses were invented.

The Kingdom of Japan invaded Korea in 1592, beginning a six-year conflict that brought incredible destruction and bloodshed. Korea eventually triumphed with the aid of China's Ming dynasty. Multiple invasions by the Chinese Manchu followed. This forced the Choson to build its own strength beyond Chinese influence.

The Choson dynasty enjoyed capable leadership and economic growth during the next two centuries. Christianity was introduced in 1784. It was later outlawed under King Taewongun in 1864. Japan forced the Choson dynasty to sign a trade treaty in 1876. Korea did not want to be locked into a relationship with Japan alone, so it signed other trade agreements with European nations and the United States.

Korea was forced to let Japanese troops use its peninsula as a route into Manchuria when Japan went to war against Russia in 1904. Japan unexpectedly defeated Russia, but its troops remained in place. It named Korea as a Japanese protectorate the following year. Eventually, it exerted more and more control over the kingdom. The peninsula was annexed by Japan in 1910, ending the Choson dynasty.

Korea both suffered and benefited under Japanese control. A network of railways was developed, communications upgraded, modern factories constructed and major exploitation of rich mineral deposits began. Liberation groups worked to expel the Japanese, but they were weak and disorganized. Millions of Koreans took part in a peaceful demonstration in 1919. This was called the March First Movement. The expected foreign

A Seoul vegetable stall.

The business district of Seoul.

support did not materialize and the Japanese merely tightened their hold.

The Allied forces began planning for the withdrawal of Japanese troops from Korea prior to the end of World War II. The United Nations divided Korea into two zones of occupation at the 38th parallel. Soviet troops occupied the north, Americans the south. Each worked to gain cooperation from citizens while dealing with the removal of the Japanese. Koreans hoped for unification, but the U. S. and the Soviet Union began arranging separate governments in 1947.

The Soviet Union vetoed all U.N. moves for reunification and free elections. All trade and travel between the two zones ceased as Cold War tensions grew. The Korean economy was in chaos. The north had the industries and mineral resources, the south had the agriculture. Desperate Koreans tried to escape communism by fleeing south.

Two separate states, the Democratic People's Republic of Korea (North Korea) and the Republic of Korea (South Korea) were established in 1948. Kim Il Sung emerged as leader of North Korea. All foreign troops were withdrawn from both

countries during 1949. The Soviet Union ensured North Korea had its own large, well-equipped army, unlike the South.

North Korean troops crossed the 38th parallel into the South on June 25, 1950. United States President Harry Truman mobilized U.S. forces. The United Nations assembled an multinational coalition to defend South Korea, commanded by General Douglas MacArthur.

The North Koreans met little resistance from the South Korean army and a small U.S. force. The North Koreans had pushed their opponents into an area around Pusan by Septem-

South Korea

ELECTRA COLLECTION

The United Nations landing force at Inchon.

ber 10, 1950. On September 15, 1950 MacArthur staged a highly successful landing at Inchon. The invaders began withdrawing. They returned to North Korea by September 27th.

The United Nations forces pursued them into the North. By late November, despite the bitter winter, they had reached the Yalu River, the border between Korea and China. A vast Chinese army stormed into North Korea, scattering the United Nations forces. The communists had taken Seoul, the capital of South Korea by January of 1951.

The United Nations tried to negotiate a cease-fire through peace talks. Fighting continued because the Soviets would not agree to the U. N. terms for the peaceful exchange of prisoners. A truce was finally signed on July 27, 1953.

The truce was signed at the village of Panmunjom, close to the 38th parallel. Huge numbers of United States troops remained in South Korea. It continues to be a key base for the U.S. military.

South Korea's first president was Syngman Rhee. He was elected by a legislature formed under U. S. authorities and sanctioned by the United Nations.

South Korea had been the site of most of the peninsula's agriculture. It had no major industries. Its natural resources beyond farmland had yet to be developed. Unemployment was very high and inflation almost out of control.

Rhee's government struggled through the 1950s, weighed down by accusations of corruption and brutality. The highly contested elections of 1960 prompted large protests. Rhee was forced from office and went into exile when 125 students were shot by police.

Rhee's successor, Chang Myun, enacted liberalizing reforms of many types. The armed forces seized power in a *coup d'état* the following year. They were led by General Park Chung Hee. Personal freedoms were severely suppressed by the military. Park Chung Hee was elected president in 1963.

The Park government reduced corruption and developed industry rapidly. Park placed South Korea under martial law in October of 1972. He introduced a new constitution enabling him to remain president indefinitely. Park was assassinated in October of 1979 by his own secret police chief. The new president, Choi Kyu Hah, increased the violent suppression of his predecessor.

Serious civil unrest followed Park's death. Workers and students united in a popular uprising in Kwangju in May 1980. The military reacted with

**The Bell Pavilion
in central Seoul.**

SCOTT BRODIE

astounding brutality, killing more than two hundred protestors.

Chun Doo Hwan took over the presidency in 1980. Another new constitution was adopted. Martial law was lifted in January 1981. Chun's Democratic Justice Party won a majority in the National Assembly in March 1981. Nakasone Tashiro, Japan's prime minister, pledged $4 billion in low-interest loans to aid South Korean economic development.

Tensions rose in 1983 when the Soviet Union shot down a South Korean passenger jet which had strayed into its air space. All 269 people onboard were killed. Korea demanded an apology, but the Soviet

Union insisted the jet was on a spy mission.

Chun began releasing opponents from jail, under international pressure. The New Korea Democratic Party (NKDP) was formed by Kim Dae Jung and Kim Young Sam, two of the most prominent people released from prison. The NKDP became the main opposition in the February 1985 elections. The border with North Korea was opened for family visits in 1986. This was the first time such privileges had been granted since the war ended in 1954.

Chun Doo Huan promised democratic reforms following widespread protests in 1987.

FLAT EARTH PICTURE GALLERY

**Women in traditional
Korean dress at Taejon.**

He agreed to the direct election of the president. Roh Tae Woo was elected president the following December. A new constitution was adopted in 1988. Both South Korea and North Korea joined the United Nations in 1991. The two nations signed a nonagression pact three months later.

The 1992 election of Kim Young Sam marked a profound change for Korea. He was the first non-military figure to occupy the leadership for more than thirty years. He immediately curbed the military's power and the economic power of Korea's family-controlled industries.

In 1996, Former presidents Chun Doo Huan and Roh Tae Woo were indicted for corruption, fraud and the 1980 mur-

South Korea

der of protestors at Kwangju. Chun was sentenced to death. His sentence was later commuted to life imprisonment. Roh was sentenced to seventeen years imprisonment. This victory for the people was tainted when both were granted amnesty and freed from prison in 1997.

Korea plunged into economic chaos as recession swept across Asia in 1997. The South Korean currency dropped fifty percent in value, while the stock market declined sixty

Guarding the truce village at Panmunjom.

percent. President Kim Young Sam was badly discredited by both the economic situation and family corruption scandals. He was defeated in early 1998 by Kim Dae Jung.

The new president agreed to an International Monetary Fund recovery plan despite fierce opposition. Signs of improvement were evident by 1999. Econonic recovery continues at a slow but steady rate.

One of Kim Dae Jung's primary concerns was the reunification talks which had occurred intermittenly since 1972. An historic meeting took place between Kim Dae Jung and Kim Jong Il of North Korea in June of 2000. The two leaders signed a declaration that endorsed the goals of reconciliaton and reunification. They pledged to increase cooperation on economic, cultural, humanitarian and other issues. This effort and his longtime commitment to democracy and human rights won Kim Dae Jung the Nobel Peace Prize in 2000.

The Nandaemun Gate , part of the ancient city of Seoul.

Kuwait

STATE OF KUWAIT

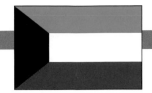

Situated on the northwestern coast of the Persian Gulf, Kuwait is a tiny nation occupying only about 7,000 square miles (app. 17,000 sq km). This area includes the mainland and a number of offshore islands, the largest of which is Bubiyan. Ninety percent of Kuwait's landscape is stony desert on a low-lying plateau. The region receives very little rain and is hot and dry most of the year. Temperatures in Kuwait often exceed 115°F. (46.1° C.) during the summer.

Almost all of Kuwait's population lives near the Gulf coastline. Approximately eighty percent are Arabs, half of whom are Kuwaiti nationals. There is a large population of guest workers from southern Asian countries. Around eighty-five percent of the people are Muslim, the majority of which are Sunnite. Most of the others are Christian or Hindu. Arabic is the official language, but English is also spoken.

The trading port of Kuwait town was established in 1716 by the Bani Utub people. They were closely related to the Unayzah tribes of central Arabia. It prospered and by 1756 was controlled by the al-Sabah family. The region was loosely controlled by the Turkish Ottoman Empire during the latter part of the nineteenth century.

Kuwaiti emir Mubarak al-Sabah opted to accept British protection in 1899. He wanted to put an end to increasing control by the Ottomans. Britain continued its protective role even after granting Kuwait its independence in 1914. The Saudi Arabian province of Najd attacked Kuwait shortly thereafter. Peace was restored with the help of the British in 1921. A new boundary between Kuwait and Najd was established with the signing of a treaty the following year.

The discovery of oil in 1938 led to the establishment of the Kuwait Oil Company. It was a partnership between British Petroleum and Gulf Oil. The emir of Kuwait shared equally in the company's profits.

The British protectorate of Kuwait Kuwait ended in June of 1961. Iraq immediately renewed its long-standing claim that Kuwait was part of its territory. Kuwait once again requested British troops, which began occupation in July of that year. Iraq relented until May 1973 when it occupied a Kuwaiti border post. Iraq withdrew following a military clash.

The Kuwaiti government gained complete control of the Kuwait Oil Company. It established the Kuwait Petroleum Corp. in 1980. Kuwait aided Iraq during the Iran-Iraq war of the 1980s. Iran threatened to attack Kuwait's shipping fleet

Kuwait

LONELY PLANET IMAGES — CHRIS MELLOR

Kuwait Towers, used for water storage and as an observation point.

countries, was formed to take military action against Iraq. The Iraqis destroyed much of Kuwait City before the coalition forces drove them out in 1991. They also sabotaged and set fire to as many as 700 Kuwaiti oil wells. The region suffered major environmental consequences as well as the economic cost.

The people of Kuwait suffered from lack of food, water and electricity after the war. Friction continued between those who stayed to fight the Iraqis and those who fled the country. Rebuilding the economy was the priority through the 1990s. The emir issued an edict giving women the right to vote in 1999. The National Assembly refused to ratify it. The United Nations approved a $15.9 billion claim brought by Kuwait against Iraq for damages to its oil fields during the war.

Forces led by the U. S. and Britain attacked the government of Saddam Hussein of Iraq in March and April of 2003. Kuwait provided invaluable support for this effort, largely in terms of the use of its land and air space for military operations. Kuwait offered $100 million in food and medicines to the people of Iraq at the end of that confrontation.

in 1987, but was repelled by military forces from the U. S. and the Soviet Union.

Iraqi president Saddam Hussein accused Kuwait of flooding the world oil market and forcing the price down in 1989. His troops stormed into Kuwait on August 2, 1990. The royal family fled the country, leaving their people to face a variety of human rights' abuses by Iraqi troops. Kuwait City was badly looted by the Iraquis. Stolen property was shipped to Iraq.

A coalition of nations, including the United States and various European and Arab

Kyrgyzstan

KYRGYZ REPUBLIC

Kyrgyzstan is located in the eastern part of central Asia. It is located at the juncture of two mountain systems, the Tien Shan and the Pamirs. Most of the country is mountainous. There is a huge variation in climate across Kyrgyzstan.

Kyrgyzstan is home to more than eighty ethnic groups. The largest, the Kyrgyz, makes up half the country's population. Other substantial groups include Russians, Uzbeks, Ukranians, Tatars, Tajiks and Kazakhs. Most are Sunni Muslims. Kyrgyz and Russian are the official languages.

Kyrgyzstan's head of state is the president, elected by the people to a five-year term. Members of the two houses of its legislature are also popularly elected for five years. The head of government is the prime minister, who is chosen by the president with the approval of the legislature.

The nomadic Kyrgyz tribe moved west to settle in this region in the sixteenth century. The Oirots, a Mongolian people, conquered the area in the late seventeenth century. The Kokand Khanate took over in the early nineteenth century. Russia sent troops to conquer Kyrgyzstan in the 1850s. They were finally successful in 1876.

The Kyrgyz people remained fiercely independent despite the Russian control.

Local guerrilla groups fought the communist Red Army for control following the Russian Revolution of 1917. They were unsuccessful. The aftermath of war was a famine in which 500,000 died. Kyrgyzstan was grouped with Soviet Turkestan and made part of the Russian Empire 1921.

The region became the Kyrgyz Autonomous Republic in 1926. It was incorporated into the Soviet Union as a full republic ten years later. Nationalism was ruthlessly suppressed by Stalin in the 1930s.

Kyrgyzstan distanced itself from Russian dominance following reforms introduced by the Soviet Union's Mikhail Gorbachev in the 1980s. It declared itself independent in August of 1991 and became a member of the Confederation of Independent States later that year. Askar Akayev was elected president.

Kyrgyzstan's government became one of the most liberal and open in the region. Agricultural land was privatized in 1998. Akayev's rule had grown more autocratic as the 1990s ended. He was nonetheless reelected in 2000. The 2000 elections were marred by accusations of corruption. Kyrgyzstan offered the use of its Manas Airport to the United States military as a base in its 2001 war against terrorism.

Laos

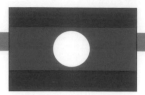

Laos is a long, narrow country is Southeast Asia. It is bordered by China, Vietnam, Cambodia, Thailand and Myanmar. Much of the country is mountains which run from north to south. The eastern border is heavily forested as is much of the Mekong River valley of the west. The climate is tropical, with high temperatures all through the year. The rainy season occurs between May and October.

The population is made up of the Lao-Loum, Lao-Theung and the Lao-Soung. Most Laotians are Theravada Buddhists. The Lao-Theung follow traditional animist religions. Lao is the official language.

Laos was founded by immigrants from China between the sixth and thirteenth centuries. The Lang Xang kingdom was formed in the mid-fourteenth century by Prince Fa Ngum. His wife, a former Khmer princess, encouraged him to adopt Buddhism as the religion of the kingdom. Lang Xang expanded into Burma, Siam (Thailand), Vietnam and Cambodia over the next 300 years.

Siam and Vietnam conquered large sections of the much-weakened Lang Xang kingdom in the eighteenth century. France expelled Siam and made Laos part of French Indochina in the late 1880s.

Japan occupied the country during World War II. An independence movement called Lao Issarak declared Laos independent after Japan's surrender to the Allies. King Sisavang Vong, however, permitted the French to return. The anti-French, pro-communist Pathet Lao movement, led by Prince Souphanouvong, established a government in the north in 1953. Prince Souvanna Phouma controlled the south. France withdrew in 1954.

The princes formed a coalition in 1957. It collapsed following the withdrawal of United States aid. Laos was divided between the Pathet Lao (Lao State) in the north and a right-wing government in the south in 1960. A 1962 cease-fire lasted a year.

The Pathet Lao was heavily supported by the communist North Vietnamese government. The United States began bombing Laos in 1964, in pursuit of North Vietnamese forces. The Pathet Lao controlled two-thirds of the country by the 1967 cease-fire. The following year Souvanna Phouma formed a coalition government.

The Pathet Lao took control following communist victories in Vietnam and Cambodia in 1975. Large numbers of people fled to Thailand. Laos developed a more market-based economy by the 1990s. Presidential powers were increased in 1991. Laotians are rigidly controlled by the government.

GOVERNMENT
Capital Vientiane
Type of government
Communist republic
Independence from France
July 19, 1949
Voting
Universal adult suffrage, compulsory
Head of state President
Head of government Prime Minister
Constitution 1991
Legislature
Unicameral National Assembly
Judiciary People's Supreme Court
Member of
ASEAN, IMF, UN, UNESCO, WHO

LAND AND PEOPLE
Land area 91,429 sq mi
(236,800 sq km)
Highest point Phou Bia
9,252 ft (2,820 m)
Population 5,777,180
Major cities and populations
Vientiane 640,000
Savannaket 55,000
Ethnic groups Lao-Loum 68%,
Lao-Theung 22%, Lao-Soung 9%
Religions
Buddhism 60%, traditional animism 30%, Christianity 2%
Languages
Lao (official),
French, English

ECONOMIC
Currency Kip
Industry
mining, timber, agricultural processing, garments, tourism
Agriculture
sweet potatoes, vegetables, corn, coffee, sugar cane, cotton, tea, peanuts, rice, livestock, poultry
Natural resources
timber, gypsum, tin, gold, gemstones

Latvia

REPUBLIC OF LATVIA

Latvia is located in northern Europe on the Baltic Sea coast. It is relatively low-lying, with many swamps and lakes of various sizes. The fertile plains are drained by several major rivers. Nearly fifty percent of the country is forested. Summers are cool to warm. Winters can be very cold.

About half of the population is of Latvian descent. Russians make up most of the balance. There are small communities of Belarussians, Poles and Ukranians. Latvian is the official language although many people speak Russian.

Latvia's economy depends largely on agriculture, fishing, and wood products industries. It is an important producer of consumer goods, such as radios and washing machines. The economy is closely tied to those of Estonia, Lithuania, and other former European Soviet republics.

The Lettish people inhabited Latvia in the ninth century A.D. Germany, followed by Poland and Russia, dominated beginning in the thirteenth century. Christianity was adopted during this time. The Teutonic Knights of Livonia controlled Latvia from 1237 to 1561. Poland gained control through 1621, at which time Sweden conquered much of Latvia. Russia controlled all of the country by 1795.

Latvian nationalists declared independence on November 18, 1918. Efforts by Russian troops to regain control were thwarted by Allied forces. A republican constitution was proclaimed in 1922, with Karlis Ulmanis as president. Land reform concentrated on dividing large estates into smaller parcels for more Latvians.

Shaky coalition governments and economic problems provoked a *coup d'état* in 1934. Ulmanis took power as a dictator. Latvia signed a mutual-assistance treaty with the USSR at the outbreak of World War II. The USSR, however, suspected Latvia of forming an anti-Soviet alliance with Estonia. The Soviets invaded in June of 1940. A Communist regime was installed. The Latvian Soviet Socialist Republic was created on July 21, 1940.

Latvia became part of the Soviet Union in 1944. Farming had been collectivized and rapid industrialization had begun by the 1950s.

Pro-independence, non-communist Latvian Popular Front candidates gained power in the 1988 elections. They restored the constitution of 1922, making Latvia independent. Despite Soviet opposition, the people confirmed the changes on March 3, 1991. The Communist Party was banned and all Russian troops left the country within three years.

Lebanon

REPUBLIC OF LEBANON

Lebanon is located on the eastern coast of the Mediterranean Sea, in far south-western Asia. Beyond the narrow coastal plain is the Jabal Lubnan, or Lebanon Mountains. They run from north to south for the full length of the country. East of the mountains is the fertile Bekaa Valley. The Anti-Lebanon Mountains are in the west at the border with Syria. Lebanon has long, hot summers with little rainfall. Most rain falls during the short winters.

All but five percent of the population are Arabs. Small groups of Armenians, Kurds, Greeks, Assyrians and Turks also live in Lebanon. Lebanon has a significant Christian population, at around twenty-five percent. Most of the balance is either Shi'ite or Sunni Muslim. Arabic is the official language. Many people speak French or English.

Canaanites established the Phoenician Empire in what is now Lebanon and Syria in ancient times. Lebanon was controlled by the Persian Empire after 500 B.C. and was later conquered by Alexander the Great. Rome conquered the region in 64 B.C.

Maronite Christians settled in the northern mountains in the seventh century A.D. Islam was introduced in 630 following the Arab conquest. The Druses, an extremist Shi-ite Muslim sect, established themselves some time later. The area also had a significant Jewish population. These differences laid the basis for the religious strife which continues today.

Lebanon was overrun by Christian crusaders from Europe beginning in about 1100. Lebanon, or the Levant as it was commonly known, became a major trading center with close links to Europe. The Ottoman Turks conquered the region in 1516.

A civil war in the late 1850s between Muslims and Christians took many lives. The Ottomans and other European powers intervened to end the fighting and to punish the Muslims for instigating battle. France was given a League of Nations mandate over Syria and Lebanon after World War I. Predominantly Christian Lebanon was made a semi-autonomous republic in 1926.

Christian and Muslim leaders declared independence during World War II. France reluctantly agreed in 1943.

A United Nations mine removal team working in southern Lebanon in the early 1990s.

UNITED NATIONS PHOTO LIBRARY

Lebanon became an independent republic on January 1, 1944. There was an unwritten agreement that the government structure would reflect the country's religious components.

Lebanese troops participated in the 1949 war against Israel. It maintained close relations with the West, although acceptance of United States aid led to rioting in 1958. United States forces quelled the growing rebellion at President Camille Chamoun's request.

The situation eased when General Fouad Chehab was elected president. Lebanon became a major commercial and distribution center for the region. Beirut attracted many international banking and trading organizations.

Lebanon did not participate in the 1967 war against Israel. It was, however, used by militants seeking a Palestinian homeland. Israel raided their bases during 1968. The Lebanese army attempted to suppress the Palestinians' activities the following year.

Lebanon was embroiled in a Christian–Muslim civil war by 1975. In April the following year, at the government's request, Syrian forces intervened to suppress the Muslims. Lebanon's formerly successful economy had been shattered.

Israeli forces occupied South Lebanon in 1978 and 1982 following attacks by Palestine Liberation Organization (PLO) guerrillas. A U.N. peacekeeping force was sent to the region.

President Bashir Gemayel was assassinated in 1982. Christian Falangist militia massacred 1000 Palestinian refugees shortly thereafter. More than 300 U. S. and French troops were killed in terrorist bombings on October 23, 1983. The Western forces then left the area. Christian and Muslim militias maintained their civil war. Shi'ite militia groups began kidnapping Westerners in Beirut with Iran's support.

Syrian forces occupied the Muslim sector of Beirut in 1987. A new constitution gave more power to Muslims. President René Moawad was assassinated after 17 days in office. Syrians aided the Lebanese army in regaining control over much of the country after ousting the PLO from southern strongholds.

The last of the Western hostages was released in 1992. Attempts to disarm the militias were proving successful. South Lebanon, however, remained a battleground. Clashes between Shi'ite Hezbollah guerrillas and the Israeli army continued through the 1990s.

Attempts are being made to rebuild Lebanon's shattered economy and bring some normalcy to national life. Israel withdrew from South Lebanon in 2000. Syria continues to play a major role in Lebanon's government and policies.

GOVERNMENT
Capital Beirut
Type of government Republic
**Independence from France
(UN Trust Territory)**
January 1, 1944
Voting
Universal adult male suffrage,
partial adult female suffrage
Head of state President
Head of government Prime Minister
Constitution
1926, numerous amendments
Legislature
Unicameral National Assembly
Judiciary Courts of Cassation
Member of AAL, IMF, UN,
UNESCO, UNHCR, WHO

LAND AND PEOPLE
Land area 4,036 sq mi
(10,452 sq km)
Highest point
Qurnat as Sawda 10,115 ft (3,083 m)
Coastline 140 mi (225 km)
Population 3,677,780
Major cities and populations
Beirut 1,600,000
Ethnic groups
Arab 95%, others 5%
Religions Islam 70%, Christianity 25%
Languages
Arabic (official), French, English

ECONOMIC
Currency Lebanese pound
Industry
banking, food processing, jewellery, cement, textiles, mining, chemicals, wood products, oil refining
Agriculture
citrus, grapes, tomatoes, apples, vegetables, potatoes, olives, sheep
Natural resources
limestone, iron ore, salt, water

Lesotho

KINGDOM OF LESOTHO

The kingdom of Lesotho is a landlocked nation in southern Africa. The western lowlands are the most fertile area. The Orange River, which originates in Lesotho, runs through these plains. The landscape rises in the east to the great heights of the Drakensburg Mountains. The climate is subtropical, with cool winters and hot summers.

Virtually all of the population are Sotho people. Minorities include the Zulu, Fingo and Tembu. Twenty percent of the population observes traditional indigenous religions, while most of the others are Christians. Sesotho and English are the official languages of the nation.

The San people originally inhabited Lesotho. They were gradually displaced by the Besotho people in the eighteenth century. The Besotho, under King Moshesh, faced many invasions by the Zulus in the early nineteenth century. King Moshesh introduced Christianity in partnership with European missionaries. The Boers attacked the kingdom in 1838, after which the king asked Britain to make his land a protectorate. Basutoland, as it became known, was annexed to the Cape Colony in 1868.

The Union of South Africa was established in 1910. Basutoland resisted incorporation into it because of its institution of apartheid, a policy of racial segregation.

Lesotho remained a British territory until its independence was declared on October 4, 1966. Head of state was King Moshoeshoe II and the prime minister was Chief Leabua Jonathan.

Jonathan declared a state of emergency after his defeat in the 1970 general elections. He suspended the constitution and the parliament, taking absolute power. Jonathan retained power until 1986 when he was deposed in a coup. King Moshoeshoe was given executive power. The king went into exile after disagreements with the military. His son became monarch King Letsie II in 1990.

During the 1970s and 1980s Lesotho had opposed South Africa because of apartheid. South Africa blockaded trade and transport routes as a result. It later staged military raids into the country.

Lesotho returned to civilian rule in 1993, with a new constitution and parliament and free elections. Ntsu Mokhehle became prime minister.

Prime Minister Mokhele left office to found the Lesotho Congress for Democracy in 1997. New elections were held in 1998. Violent riots followed accusations of election fraud. South African and Botswanian troops entered Lesotho to restore order.

GOVERNMENT
Website www.lesotho.gov.ls
Capital Maseru
Type of government
Constitutional monarchy
Independence from Britain
October 4, 1966
Voting Universal adult suffrage
Head of state Monarch
Head of government Prime Minister
Constitution 1993
Legislature
Bicameral Parliament
Assembly (lower house),
Senate (upper house)
Judiciary High Court
Member of CN, IMF, OAU, UN, UNESCO, UNHCR, WHO, WTO

LAND AND PEOPLE
Land area 11,720 sq mi
(30,355 sq km)
Highest point
Thabana Ntlenyana
11,282 ft (3,482 m)
Population 2,207,954
Major cities and populations
Maseru 295,000
Ethnic groups
Sotho 85%, Zulu 10%
Religions
Christianity 80%, traditional animism 20%
Languages
Sesotho, English (both official), indigenous languages

ECONOMIC
Currency Loti
Industry
food, beverages, textiles, clothing assembly, handicrafts
Agriculture
corn, wheat, pulses, sorghum, barley, livestock
Natural resources
water, diamonds, minerals

Liberia

REPUBLIC OF LIBERIA

GOVERNMENT
Website www.micat.gov.lr
Capital Monrovia
Type of government Republic
Voting Universal adult suffrage
Head of state President
Head of government President
Constitution 1986
Legislature
Bicameral National Assembly
House of Representatives (lower
house), Senate (upper house)
Judiciary Supreme Court
Member of
IMF, OAU, UN, UNESCO, WHO

LAND AND PEOPLE
Land area 37,743 sq mi
(97,754 sq km)
Highest point Mount Wuteve
4,471 ft (1,380 m)
Coastline 370 mi (579 km)
Population 3,288,198
Major cities and populations
Monrovia 900,000
Ethnic groups Indigenous African
95%, American-Liberian 5%
Religions Traditional animism
70%, Islam 20%, Christianity 10%
Languages
English (official), indigenous
languages

ECONOMIC
Currency Liberian dollar
Industry
rubber processing, palm oil
processing, timber, mining
Agriculture
rubber, coffee, cacao, rice, tapioca,
palm oil, sugar cane, bananas,
sheep, goats, timber
Natural resources
iron ore, timber, diamonds, gold

Liberia is on the western coast of Africa. Its narrow coastal strip features numerous lagoons and mangroves. Inland from the coast lies rugged plateau country, rising to mountains near the Guinea border. The climate is equatorial, with consistently high temperatures and humidity.

Indigenous African peoples, including the Malinke, Gola, Grebo and Kru, make up most of Liberia. Most people follow traditional animist religions. English is the official language, but tribal dialects are widely used.

The mining of iron ore replaced rubber production as the country's primary industry in the early 1960s. Civil war broke out in the mid-1990s, virtually destroying most facets of the country's economy.

Liberia was founded in 1822 by the American Colonization Society as a home for freed slaves. The capital, Monrovia, was named for United States President Monroe. The Republic of Liberia was formed on July 26, 1847.

Liberia joined the Allies during World War I. Firestone Corporation opened a large rubber plantation there in 1926.

The League of Nations found that Liberian companies were exploiting forced labor in the early 1930s. The scandal caused the president to resign. The new government of 1936 changed laws and improved the country's global standing.

President William Tubman began encouraging foreign investment in 1944. He made it possible for more Liberians to participate in the political system. Liberia was a founding member of the U.N. in 1945.

W.R. Tolbert became president upon the death of Tubman in 1971. Economic tensions led to fierce riots in 1979. Tolbert was killed the following year. The People's Redemption Council, led by Samuel Doe, took control. A bloody crackdown on opponents provoked coups during the early 1980s. Government corruption and human rights abuses strained relations with the U.S. by the late 1980s.

Charles Taylor's National Patriotic Front led an uprising against the government in 1989. President Doe was assassinated. More than 150,000 people were killed in the ensuing civil war. Over a million others fled their homes. A multinational peacekeeping force was sent to Liberia, but Taylor resisted. He was aided by Libya and Burkina Faso.

Taylor won the 1997 elections. The fighting continued. Taylor's government was accused of arming rebels in Sierra Leone in return for diamonds in 2000. The U.N. imposed sanctions on Liberia in 2001 for its refusal to end ties to the rebels.

Libya

LONELY PLANET IMAGES – JANE SWEENEY

A street in the Medina in the city of Tripoli.

Libya is in northern Africa on the Mediterrean Sea. All but five percent of its land is rocky, barren and arid. The land rises to mountains near the southern border with Chad. The Mediterranean coastline gets a small amount of rain, while most of the country gets hardly any. The climate is marked by extreme daytime heat and cool nights.

The southern deserts are home to small groups of nomadic Tebou and Tuareg peoples. The rest of the population are of Arab or Berber descent, with small communities of Greeks, Italians, Egyptians, Pakistanis, Turks and Tunisians. Almost all are Sunni Muslims. About two percent are Christian with a tiny Jewish minority. Arabic is the official language although Berber Hamitic is widely spoken.

Phoenician traders established Tripolitania on the Libyan coast around 700 B.C. Cyrenaica was later settled by Greeks. Both were conquered by Alexander the Great. For 500 years, from 200 B.C., it came under Roman control. Vandals conquered Libya in the fifth century A.D.

A brief period of control by the Byzantine Empire ended with the Arab invasion of 643. Ruled successively by the Umayyads, Fatimids and a Berber dynasty, part of the country was conquered by the Normans in 1146. The Almohads from Morocco controlled it for a while, followed by several others during the next centuries.

The Ottoman Empire arrived in the sixteenth century. Control was loose and the area was semi-autonomous. It became a haven for pirates preying on merchant vessels in the Mediterranean. The Ottomans tolerated the hereditary ruling family until 1835, when it was deposed.

Italy, seeking a colonial empire, invaded Libya in 1911. Widespread resistance lasted until 1931 despite the surrender of the Ottoman governor.

Libya saw major desert battles during World War II. Italian

and Germany armies fought the Allied troops. The Allies expelled the Axis troops from Libya in 1943.

Libya came under an Anglo–French military government until 1949. The United Nations then took over and granted independence. The United Kingdom of Libya was established on December 24, 1951. King Idris I was its head of government. Libya joined the Arab League in 1953 and the U.N. in 1955.

Great Britain and the U.S. pledged economic aid to Libya in exchange for a continued military presence there. The last British and U. S. troops stationed in Libya were withdrawn in 1970.

Libya was a very poor country until the discovery of oil in the mid-1950s. The economy began to boom as the oil industry developed.

The king was deposed by army officers in 1969. The army was led by Colonel Muammar al-Qaddafi. Qadhafi's political philosophy was a mixture of Islam and socialism. He decreed that all businesses should be nationalized. Libya soon took control of the country's oil resources.

Libya began to take a more active role in international politics. Qadhafi supported the efforts of the Palestine Liberation Army. He began a systematic purge of his opponents following a coup attempt in 1975. Many who fled to other countries were pursued and executed. Their murders on foreign soil generated widespread condemnation.

Libyan relations with the United States deteriorated in the 1980s. Libya's connection to terrorist attacks in Italy in 1985 led to clashes between Libyan and U.S. Navy units in the Gulf of Sidra. The U.S. later bombed sites believed to be terrorist centers in Libya. Qadhafi began taking a more subdued position. A number of terrorist groups were expelled.

Libyans were believed to be involved in the bombings of two Western civilian aircraft in 1988 and 1989. Britain issued extradition warrants for suspects. Libya refused to comply.

Indications that Libya was manufacturing chemical weapons prompted United Nations sanctions in 1992. With its economy in a dire condition, Libya agreed to hand over the Pan Am bombing suspects in 1999. They were tried in the Netherlands under Scottish law. The country had suffered a $30 billion loss from sanctions up to this point. The United Nations sanctions were lifted, but those of the United States were not.

The Libyan government was restructured in 2000. Regional and local bodies now have more power. Qaddafi continues to control security, foreign policy and the oil industry.

GOVERNMENT
Capital Tripoli
Type of government Military dictatorship
Independence from UN Trust Territory status December 24, 1951
Voting Universal adult suffrage, compulsory
Head of state Revolutionary Leader
Head of government Secretary of the General People's Committee
Constitution 1969
Legislature Unicameral General People's Assembly
Judiciary Supreme Court
Member of AL, IMF, OAU, OPEC, UN, UNESCO, WHO

LAND AND PEOPLE
Land area 679,360 sq mi (1,759,540 sq km)
Highest point Bikku Bitti 7,438 ft (2267 m)
Coastline 1,100 mi (1770 km)
Population 5,500,000
Major cities and populations Tripoli 1,800,000 Benghazi 800,000
Ethnic groups Arab-Berber 97%, others 3%
Religions Islam 97%, Christianity 2%
Languages Arabic (official)

ECONOMIC
Currency Libyan dinar
Industry petroleum, food processing, textiles, handicrafts, cement
Agriculture wheat, barley, olives, dates, citrus, vegetables, peanuts, soybeans, cattle
Natural resources petroleum, natural gas, gypsum

Liechtenstein

PRINCIPALITY OF LIECHTENSTEIN

The tiny Principality of Liechtenstein occupies only 62 square miles (160 sq km). It lies between Switzerland and Austria in central Europe. Liechtenstein's western edge lies in the valley of the Rhine River. Most of the rest of the country is the foothills of the Alps. The summers, under the influence of a southerly wind, are warm. Winters can be very cold.

Most of the people are of Alemannic origin, a branch of early Germans. Christianity is the religion of almost all Liechtensteiners. German is the official language, although it has been modified into a unique Alemannish dialect.

The principality's liberal tax laws have promoted huge income from international banking, tourism and the sale of postage stamps. Liechtenstein is highly industrialized, producing machinery, pharmaceuticals, precision instruments, textiles, pottery and food products.

The counties of Vaduz and Schellenberg were acquired by the Liechtenstein family in 1719. This family, which came from an Austrian background, allied themselves with the Habsburg dynasty during the 18th and 19th centuries. Liechtenstein declared itself a neutral country, a position it maintains today. This neutrality was respected by both sides during World Wars I and II.

The Habsburg dynasty was abolished after World War I. Liechtenstein formed its present connection with Switzerland. Prince Franz Joseph, who became head of state in 1938, yielded authority to his son, Prince Hans-Adam II in 1984.

A referendum in 1984 granted women the right to vote in parliamentary elections. The principality continues to be ruled by a hereditary dynasty. Prince Hans Adam II regularly finds himself in conflict with the elected parliament over economic policy.

A picturesque mountain village in Liechtenstein.

GOVERNMENT
Website www.fuerstenhaus.li
Capital Vaduz
Type of government
Constitutional monarchy
Voting Universal adult suffrage
Head of state Monarch
Head of government Prime Minister
Constitution 1921
Legislature
Unicameral Parliament (Landtag)
Judiciary Supreme Court
Member of CE, UN, WHO

LAND AND PEOPLE
Land area
62 sq mi (160 sq km)
Highest point Grauspitz
8,527 ft (2,599 m)
Population 32,842
Major cities and populations
Schaan 5,250
Vazuz 5,100
Ethnic groups
Liechtensteiner 95%, others 5%
Religions Christianity 88%,
Islam 3%
Languages German (official)

ECONOMIC
Currency Swiss franc
Industry
electronics, textiles, ceramics,
pharmaceuticals, food products,
precision instruments, tourism
Agriculture
wheat, barley, corn, potatoes,
livestock, dairy
Natural resources
minimal

LONELY PLANET IMAGES — MARTIN MOOS

Lithuania

REPUBLIC OF LITHUANIA

 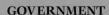
Lithuania, situated in northern Europe on the eastern shore of the Baltic Sea, has a flat landscape dotted with more than 3000 lakes. The climate is continental, its temperatures modified by proximity to the Baltic Sea. Winters are cool to cold, and summers cool to warm.

Eighty percent of the population is native Lithuanian. Most of the balance is Polish or Russian. The majority religion is Christianity, predominantly Catholic, with smaller Russian Orthodox groups. Lithuanian is the official language.

The original inhabitants settled along the banks of the River Nemen around 1500 B.C. The region was invaded by the Livonian Brothers of the Sword and the Teutonic Knights in the thirteenth century. Lithuanians united to repel them under the leadership of King Mindaugus about 1253.

Mindaugus was assassinated ten years later, but his successors conquered territory as far as Belorussia and the Ukraine. Prince Jagiello of Lithuania converted to Christianity to marry Princess Jadwiga of Poland in 1386. He was crowned Wladyslaw II Jagiello, king of Poland. The two kingdoms became closely allied. Christianity was promoted throughout the region.

Lithuania became part of Russia in 1795. The Catholic Church encouraged regular anti-Russian uprisings beginning in 1812 and lasting throughout the century.

Lithuania declared itself independent on February 16, 1918. The governments of the 1920s and 1930s were fascist dictatorships. Lithuania came under Soviet domination after the German-Soviet pact of 1939. The Lithuanian Soviet Socialist Republic was created the following year.

Rebels who resisted Germany's occupation from 1941 to 1944 also opposed the Soviets when they returned. The Soviets executed some 2,000 Lithuanians who were believed to have aided the Germans. Many others were deported to Siberia. The Soviets closed most churches and deported clergy.

The Lithuanian Reform Movement won a majority of seats in the congress in 1989. Lithuania was the first Soviet state to break with the Soviet Union. The Soviet Union granted independence to Lithuania, Estonia and Latvia on September 6, 1991. A new constitution was adopted in 1992. Algirdas Brazauskas, a former Communist, was elected president.

The 1990s brought economic struggle to the country. Some recovery has taken place in recent years. Lithuania is striving to become a member of the European Union and NATO.

Luxembourg

GRAND DUCHY OF LUXEMBOURG

Luxembourg is located in western Europe. It is bounded by Belgium, Germany and France. The heavily forested upper basins of the Sauer and Alzette rivers dominate the north. The south two-thirds of the country is a plateau called the Bon Pays. Iron ore mining takes place in the southwest, while wine production prevails in much of the southeast. The climate is continental with snowfalls in the higher regions during winter. Summers can be warm and humid.

Almost one third of Luxembourg's people are immigrants, chiefly from Portugal, Italy and other countries of Western Europe. Most others are of German or French background. Christianity is the dominant religion. Luxemburgian is the national language. German and French are widely used as well.

Luxembourg is one of the world's most highly industrialized countries. It has a high standard of living. Its once strong iron ore mining industry has weakened as resources have dwindled. Banking, manufacturing, agriculture and tourism are the mainstays of its economy.

Luxembourg was included in the province of Belgica Prima under Roman rule. The region was settled by Frankish people in the fifth century A.D. It became an autonomous country within the Holy Roman Empire during the eleventh century.

Luxembourg came under the domination of the Habsburg dynasty in 1437. For the next four centuries Spain and Austria alternately dominated the country.

Luxembourg became a grand duchy within the Kingdom of the Netherlands after the Napoleonic Wars ended in 1815. Belgium left the Netherlands in 1830, taking most of Luxembourg's territory with it. The remaining portion was recognized as an independent duchy.

German forces occupied Luxembourg at the outset of World War I. It joined the League of Nations in 1920 and it developed a strong customs and currency union with Belgium.

Germany's World War II invasion forced the government's flight to London. Germany proclaimed the duchy part of its Third Reich in 1942. Allied forces liberated Luxembourg in 1944.

Luxembourg was a founding member of the U.N. in 1945. It joined NATO in 1949 and established a customs union with Belgium and the Netherlands known as BENELUX. The European Community (now EU) began in 1958 with Luxembourg as a founding member.

The thirty-six-year reign of Grand Duke Jean ended in 2000. He was replaced by his son, Henri. Jean-Claude Juncker, at age 41, became the country's youngest prime minister in 1995.

GOVERNMENT
Website www.gouvernement.lu
Capital Luxembourg
Type of government
Constitutional monarchy
Voting
Universal adult suffrage, compulsory
Head of state Monarch
Head of government Prime Minister
Constitution 1868
Legislature
Unicameral Chamber of Deputies
Judiciary Constitutional Court
Member of CE, EU, IMF, NATO, OECD, UN, UNESCO, WHO, WTO

LAND AND PEOPLE
Land area 998 sq mi (2,586 sq km)
Highest point Buurgplaatz
1,835 ft (559 m)
Population 448,569
Major cities and populations
Luxembourg 82,000
Esch-sur-Alzette 26,000
Ethnic groups French, German
Religions Christian
Languages
Luxemburgian, French, German

ECONOMIC
Currency Euro
Industry
banking, iron, steel, food processing, chemicals, metal products, engineering, tyres, glass, aluminum
Agriculture
barley, oats, potatoes, wheat, fruits, wine grapes, livestock
Natural resources
iron ore

Macedonia

REPUBLIC OF MACEDONIA

The Republic of Macedonia, in eastern Europe, is a very mountainous country. It is divided by the vast valley of the Vardar River which runs from the northwest to southeast and drains into the Aegean Sea. Much of the country is heavily forested. Earthquakes are common. Winters are very cold and wet. Summers are usually hot and dry.

Two-thirds of the population is ethnic Macedonians. The other major group is Albanian. A majority of the people are Christian, while about thirty percent are Muslim. Macedonian is the official language.

Thracians and Illyrians inhabited the region of Macedonia as early as 2000 B.C. King Philip II unified the people of Macedonia, built a strong army and gained control of many other areas. Philip had become king of Greece by 338. B.C. Philip's son, Alexander the Great, expanded Greek–Macedonian influence across Europe and Asia. The empire was divided following Alexander's death in 323 B.C.

Rome defeated the Macedonians in 168 B.C. Macedonia became a Roman province. The Byzantine Empire gained control when the Roman Empire was divided in 395 A.D. Slavs and Bulgars took permanent control in the sixth century. The Ottoman Turks gained power in 1371.

Large numbers of Turks and Albanians migrated to Macedonia over the next five centuries, establishing numerous settlements. Greece, Serbia and Bulgaria all exercised some control over parts of the area at various times. A nationalist uprising in 1903 resulted in more than 10,000 deaths.

The country was divided among Bulgaria, Greece and Serbia following the end of the Second Balkan War in 1913. Macedonia became one of six republics making up the the Federated Socialist Republic of Yugoslavia in 1946.

The Yugoslav federation collapsed during civil war in 1991. Macedonia declared its independence and adopted its own republican constitution in September of 1991. Kiro Gligorov became its first president. The country was admitted to the United Nations in 1993.

Greece feared that the country would lay claim to Greek Macedonia. It banned Macedonian trade across its border. Macedonia redesigned its flag and reworded its constitution to please the Greeks, who then lifted the ban on trade.

Friction between Macedonians and the Albanian minority increased with the influx of about 245,000 ethnic Albanians fleeing war-torn Kosovo. U. N. and U.S. intervention led to the signing of a peace agreement in 2001.

Madagascar

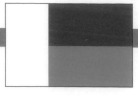

DEMOCRATIC REPUBLIC OF MADAGASCAR

Madagascar is in the Indian Ocean off the southeastern coast of Africa. The republic is made up of Madagascar, the world's fourth largest island, and several small islands. A mountainous central plateau dominates the island of Madagascar. The massive Ankaratra Mountains give way to wide fertile plains facing the Mozambique Channel in the west. Heavy rains fall between November and April. Coastal areas are warm all year round.

The people are mostly of Indonesian–Malay origin, with eighteen distinct ethnic groups. Half of the people practice animist religions. Most of the others are Christian. French and Malagasy are the official languages.

During the fifth century, immigrants from Africa and Indonesia created two distinct cultures, one inland and one on the coast. Portugese sea captain Diogo Dias, bound for India, was the first European to sight the island in 1500. France established trading settlements after 1642. Slave trading began.

Britain aided the local Merina kingdom during the eighteenth century. Merina's King Radama I permitted British missionaries to build schools and churches after 1810. Ties with Britain were severed following the king's death in 1828.

France made Madagascar a colony in 1896. Fierce resistance by locals was ruthlessly crushed. Large tracts of land were given to French settlers. Nationalist agitation grew.

A five-month revolt against France in 1947 resulted in 80,000 deaths. The independence movement continued. The island became the autonomous Malagasy Republic, within the French Community, in 1958.

The republic of Malagasy-gained independence on June 26, 1960. Philibert Tsirinana was the first president. A deteriorating economy, and Tsirinana's support for apartheid South Africa, provoked widespread demonstrations in 1972. His successor, General Gabriel Ramanantsoa, freed political prisoners and severed relations with South Africa.

Lieutenant Commander Didier Ratsiraka, president from 1975, reformed the constitution and nationalized major industries. The country's name was changed to the Republic of Madagascar.

A cholera epidemic in 1999 claimed at least 1,200 lives. Cyclones Eline and Gloria left more than 130 dead and 10,000 homeless in 2000.

The elections of 2001 were hotly contested by Ratsiraka and opponent Marc Ravalomanana. At least 70 people were killed in the ensuing civil strife. This turmoil has also seriously affected the nation's economy.

GOVERNMENT

Capital Antananarivo
Type of government Republic
Independence from France
June 26, 1960
Voting Universal adult suffrage
Head of state President
Head of government Prime Minister
Constitution 1992
Legislature
Unicameral National Assembly
Judiciary Supreme Court
Member of IMF, OAU, UN, UNESCO, UNHCR, WHO, WTO

LAND AND PEOPLE

Land area 226,658 sq mi (587,041 sq km)
Highest point Maromokotro 9,436 ft (2,876 m)
Coastline 3,000 mi (4,828 km)
Population 16,473,477
Major cities and populations
Antananarivo 1,200,000
Toamasina 130,000
Antsirabe 125,000
Ethnic groups
Merina 26%, Betsileo 12%, Betsimisaraka 15%, others 47%
Religions Traditional animism 50%, Christianity 40%, Islam 8%, others 2%
Languages
Malagasy, French (both official), indigenous languages

ECONOMIC

Currency Malagasy franc
Industry
mining, brewing, tanning, sugar refining, textiles, glassware, cement, motor vehicles, petroleum
Agriculture
coffee, vanilla, sugar cane, cloves, cacao, rice, tapioca, beans, bananas, peanuts, livestock
Natural resources
graphite, chromite, coal, bauxite, salt, quartz, tar sands, semiprecious stones, mica, seafood

Malawi

REPUBLIC OF MALAWI

GOVERNMENT
Website www.malawi.gov.mw
Capital Lilongwe
Type of government Republic
Independence from Britain
July 6, 1964
Voting Universal adult suffrage
Head of state President
Head of government President
Constitution 1994
Legislature
Unicameral National Assembly
Judiciary Supreme Court of
Appeal
Member of CN, IMF, OAU, UN,
UNESCO, WHO, WTO

LAND AND PEOPLE
Land area 45,747 sq mi
(118,484 sq km)
Highest point Sapitwa
9,849 ft (3,002 m)
Population 10,548,250
Major cities and populations
Blantyre 480,000
Lilongwe 440,000
Ethnic groups Chewa 35%,
Lomwe 8%, Yao 8%,
Nyanja 4%, others 45%
Religions Christianity 50%, Islam
20%, traditional animism 10%
Languages
Chichewa, English (both official),
indigenous languages

ECONOMIC
Currency Malawian kwache
Industry
tea, sugar refining, mining
timber products, cement
Agriculture
sugar cane, cotton, tea, corn,
potatoes, tapioca, sorghum,
livestock, nuts
Natural resources
limestone, uranium, coal, bauxite

Crossed from north to south by the Great Rift Valley, Malawi is a long, thin, landlocked country in southern Africa. Lake Nyasa, the third largest lake in Africa, lies within this deep valley. Most of the northern plateau is barren, but the southern Shire Highlands are heavily cultivated. The equatorial climate brings consistently high temperatures through much of the year.

About ninety-nine percent of the people of Malawi are native African. Christianity is dominant. There are significant Muslim and animist minorities. English and Chichewa are the official languages.

People lived near Lake Nyasa as early as 8000 B.C. The San people were joined by Bantu-speaking migrants from the first to the fourth centuries A.D. The Maravi kingdom became established in the center and south about 1500. The Ngonde kingdom of the north developed about 100 years later.

Scottish explorer and missionary David Livingstone arrived in 1859. He was shocked to find that the Yao people were already conducting slave trade. His reports brought missionaries from Scotland in 1873. The British South African Company began exploiting the region in 1884.

Britain established a protectorate over what it called Nyasaland in 1891. Coffee plantations were established in the Shire River valley. Forced participation of Africans in World War II fighting for Britain prompted a bloody uprising in 1915.

Britain created the Federation of Rhodesia and Nyasaland in 1953. The people of Nyasaland feared domination by the powerful white elites of Southern Rhodesia (now Zimbabwe). The federation ended in 1963. Nyasaland was given internal self-government.

Nyasaland, renamed Malawi, became independent on July 6, 1964. Hastings Banda, leader of the Malawi Congress Party, became president. Declared president for life in 1971, he became increasingly autocratic.

Banda maintained diplomatic ties with apartheid South Africa and Portuguese Mozambique. Malawi became a haven for anti-Marxist rebels fighting the government of Mozambique. More than 800,000 refugees from Mozambique also streamed in, threatening widespread famine.

Mass demonstrations followed criticism of Banda by Catholic bishops in 1992. A 1993 referendum adopted multi-party elections and abolished Banda's president-for-life status. He was defeated by Bakili Muluzi in 1994. Two years of failed crops caused severe food shortages in Malawi in 2002.

Malaysia

FEDERATION OF MALAYSIA

Malaysia is two distinct geographic entities in Southeast Asia. West, or peninsular, Malaysia is part of the Asian mainland. East Malaysia occupies the northern portion of the island of Borneo. Both regions are known for their rugged terrain and thick jungles. The country's highest mountain, Mount Kinabalu, is in East Malaysia. The climate is tropical, with a southwest monsoon from April to October and a northeast monsoon for the rest of the year. Rainfall is frequent and heavy.

There are three dominant ethnic groups in Malaysia. The largest, at sixty percent, is the Malays. Next are the Chinese with close to thirty percent, followed by the Indians with around seven percent. About half the population is Muslim. Most Chinese are Buddhists or Taoists while most Indians are Hindu. There is a significant Christian minority. Bahasa Malaysia is the official language.

Malaysia derives considerable revenue from farming, despite the fact that most of its land is dense jungle. Rubber is the most important crop, followed by palm oil and kernels, rice, pineapples, coconut and copra.

Most manufacturing is done in peninsular Malaysia, particularly in Selangor and Penang. Key manufactured items are electronic equipment, appliances, textiles, chemicals, building materials and processed foods. The vehicle industry is led by the locally manufactured Proton, the country's most popular car.

Malaysia is one of the world's leading suppliers of tin, although the quantities mined decreased sharply in the 1990s. Other important minerals include bauxite, iron ore, copper, ilmenite, natural gas, kaolin, silver and gold. Production of petroleum has increased steadily since the 1970s.

The 1997–98 Asian economic crisis severely affected Malaysia. The country refused International Monetary Fund support. It had to resort to tight controls on currency and capital markets. A substantial number of development projects have been postponed.

The system of government is based on the British Westminster model. The head of state is the Yang Dipertuan Agong, or paramount ruler. The office operates on a unique rotating system. A different member of the hereditary rulers of the nine royal states occupies the office every five years.

The Dewan Negara is the upper house of parliament. Some of its members are elected by the states while others are appointed by the Yang Dipertuan Agong. Members of the Dewan Rakyat, or lower house, are elected by the people. Electorates are weighted to favor Malay voters. Executive power is exercised by the prime minister, who is the

SCOTT BRODIE

An older shopping area in central Kuala Lumpur.

SCOTT BRODIE

The central mosque stands at the junction of the two rivers on which Kuala Lumpur is located.

leader of the Dewan Rakyat's majority party.

People from China made their way to the Malay peninsula by about 2000 B.C. The first traders arrived from India around 300 B. C. A number of important settlements were established soon after.

The powerful Sumatran Hindu kingdom of Srivijaya had bases on the peninsula by A.D. 750. Chola peoples from India's Coromandel Coast ejected Srivijaya in th eleventh century. Srivijaya returned in 1100 and remained for the next two hundred years.

Iskandar Shah, a Majpahit prince, created Malacca in the fourteenth century. It soon became a prominent trading port and a center for Islam. Malacca controlled most of the Malay Peninsula and parts of Sumatra within a short time.

Portuguese mariner Alfonso de Albuquerque captured Malacca in 1511, forcing the sultan to flee to Johor. Portuguese Malacca was under constant attack from the sultan. The Dutch took Malacca in 1641 as a fortress to control traffic through the Malacca Strait. Britain developed a strong trading presence in the area during the latter part of the century.

Francis Light, of the British East India Company, established a base on Prince of Wales Island (now Penang) in 1786. The company went on to found Singapore in 1819. It gained control of Malacca from the Dutch in 1824. The three ports were grouped as the Straits Settlements in 1826. Many Chinese merchants were attracted to the settlements.

James Brooke, a former East India Company soldier, fought to end the piracy which had become so rampant on the northern Borneo coast. The grateful Sultan of Brunei appointed him raja (governor) of Sarawak in 1841. Sarawak became a British protectorate

GOVERNMENT
Website www.smpke.jpm.my
Capital Kuala Lumpur
Type of government
Constitutional monarchy
Independence from Britain
August 31, 1957
Voting Universal adult suffrage
Head of state Paramount Ruler
Head of government Prime Minister
Constitution 1957
Legislature
Bicameral Parliament
House of Representatives (Dewan Rakyat), Senate (Dewan Negara)
Judiciary Federal Court
Member of APEC, ASEAN, CN, IMF, UN, UNESCO, WHO, WTO

LAND AND PEOPLE
Land area 127,320 sq mi
(329,758 sq km)
Highest point Mt. Kinabalu
13,451 ft (4,100 m)
Coastline 2,905 mi (4,675 km)
Population 22,662,365
Major cities and populations
Kuala Lumpur 1,200,000
Ipoh 400,000
Johor Bahru 330,000
Melaka 310,000
Ethnic groups Malay 60%, Chinese 28%, Indian 8%, others 4%
Religions
Islam 53%, Buddhism 18%, Taoism 12%, Christianity 9%, Hinduism 7%
Languages Bahasa Malaysia (official), indigenous languages

ECONOMIC
Currency Ringgit
Industry
rubber, oil palm processing, electronics, mining, tin smelting, timber logging, petroleum refining, agriculture processing
Agriculture
rubber, palm oil, cacao, rice, timber, coconuts, pepper
Natural resources
tin, petroleum, timber, copper, iron ore, natural gas, bauxite

Malaysia

SCOTT BRODIE

An idyllic location on the island of Langkawi.

in 1888, but the Brooke family continued to run it.

Conflicts within Malay communities and between Malays and the Chinese were nearly constant in the late nineteenth century. Merchants called on Britain to intervene. Treaties of protection were negotiated with the sultans of Perak, Johor, Selangor, Pahang and Negeri Sembilan. They were grouped as the Federated Malay States in 1896, with a central government at Kuala Lumpur. Other unfederated states accepted British protection in 1909.

Tin mining was mechanized and cultivation of rubber and palm oil expanded. Large numbers of indentured laborers were recruited from India to work on Malay plantations.

Japanese troops landed at Kota Bahru in the far northeast in December of 1941. Through December and January they relentlessly pushed the British, Australian and Indian defenders south. The peninsula and Singapore fell to Japan in early 1942. North Borneo surrendered shortly afterwards.

The Brooke family's control of Sarawak ended in 1946. The old Straits Settlements, Singapore, Malacca and Penang, were separated once again. This began a proposal for the creation of the Malayan Union and the subsequent declaration of independence. Included would be the nine sultanates plus Malacca and Penang. Malays opposed the inclusion of the latter two because those settlements had predominantly Chinese populations.

Action by communist guerrillas began in 1948. The cam-

paign for independence was masterminded by Chin Peng, secretary-general of the Communist Party. Britain brought in troops. Five thousand Chinese were resettled into fortified villages. The worst of the fighting was over by 1954.

The politically powerful Malays ensured Chinese influence was minimized as they wrote their constitution. Large tracts of land were set aside exclusively for Malays who also had favored access to civil service jobs. The head of state would be a Malay monarch. The Federation of Malaya came into being on August 31, 1957. Tunku Abdul Rahman was the first prime minister.

Malaysia was created on September 16, 1963. It included Singapore, Malaya, Sabah and Sarawak. The last two were included to balance the majority Chinese population of Singapore.

Fighting between Chinese and Malays turned swiftly into a full racial riot in Singapore in July of 1965. Twenty-three people died. Friction within the Malaysian government persisted, especially between Malay and Chinese members. The Malaysian parliament expelled Singapore in August of that year.

The government devoted substantial funds to the devel-

SCOTT BRODIE

The Malaysian national war memorial, which commemorates the struggle against communism from 1948 to 1960.

opment of manufacturing. Iron production, ship repair and cement manufacturing became strategic industries. Electronic components manufacturers from Japan and Europe were encouraged to invest in new industrial ventures.

A state of emergency was declared after riots broke out between Chinese and Malays in 1969. Four days of violence and hundreds of deaths ensued. The National Operations Council took over running the country until February 1971.

Abdul Rahman was replaced as prime minister in September

Many of Kuala Lumpur's older government buildings follow a Moorish architectural style.

1971 by Abdul Razak. The government claimed interracial strife resulted from the disparity of wealth between Chinese and Malays. New policies were adopted to reduce poverty, especially that of the Malays. They would be granted certain economic privileges, including jobs previously dominated by non-Malays.

Mahathir bin Mohamad became prime minister in 1981. During the 1980s and 1990s, he used the Internal Security Act to quell criticism of the government.

An economic boom in the 1990s fueled massive construction projects. These included a

new federal capitol at Putrajaya, an international airport at Sepang and the Bakun hydroelectric dam on the Rajang River. These projects were suspended when the ringgit dropped on international currency markets and the Kuala Lumpur stock market fell.

Mahathir imposed strict currency controls in 1998 to combat continuing inflation and to stabilize the value of the ringgit. This led to disagreements during which Anwar Ibrahim, Mahathir's deputy and heir apparent, was fired.

Ibrahim joined a reform movement and severely criticized the prime minister. He was sentenced to six years imprisonment for corruption. Protests by his supporters were ruthlessly suppressed by police. Mahathir was reelected in 1999. The economy of Malaysia has since much improved.

SCOTT BRODIE

Maldives

Maldives consists of a chain of nearly 2,000 small coral islands grouped into a cluster of atolls. The republic is located in the Indian Ocean southwest of the southernmost tip of India. Tropical vegetation presents a classic picture of an island paradise. The climate is tropical with consistently high temperatures and humidity throughout the year. Most of the 60 inches (1525 mm) of rain falls between May and November.

Maldivians are descended from Sinhalese, Arab, Dravidian and African backgrounds. Almost all are Sunni Muslims. They speak Divehi, a Sinhalese language.

It is believed that the original inhabitants were Dravidians who migrated from southern India around 400 B.C. There was a large influx of Sinhalese from Ceylon (Sri Lanka) soon afterward. They were Buddhists until 1153, when their powerful sultan decreed that his subjects must convert to Islam.

The Portuguese controlled Maldives from 1558 to 1573, administering the islands from Goa in India. The islands were controlled by Dutch rulers from Ceylon for a time in the seventeenth century. Britain gained control of Ceylon in 1796. It declared a protectorate over the islands in 1887. The sultans continued to rule with absolute authority until a new constitution delivered a more democratic regime.

An internally self-governing republic was established in 1953. It was overthrown in a coup the following year and the sultanate was resumed. Britain granted independence on July 26, 1965. Ibrahim Nasir was named prime minister. The population voted to become a republic in a 1968 referendum. Nasir became president.

Nasir's successor in 1978 was Maumoon Abdul Gayoom. He survived coup attempts in 1980, 1981 and 1988. The 1988 uprising, led by mercenaries, was put down by Indian troops. Relations with India deteriorated in the mid-1990s. Maldivians were accused of infiltrating India's secret military weapons program.

Maldives and six other countries founded the South Asian Association for Regional Cooperation (SAARC) for social and economic cooperation in 1985. Maldives received U.N. aid for research to improve productivity of its small-scale fisheries in 1991.

The greatest present concern for Maldives is global warming. A significant rise in sea levels would see many of its islands disappear. Gayoom has been vocal in international meetings, calling on large nations to reduce carbon emissions.

GOVERNMENT
Website
www.presidencymaldives.gov.mv
Capital Malé
Type of government Republic
Independence from Britain
July 26, 1965
Voting Universal adult suffrage
Head of state President
Head of government President
Constitution 1998
Legislature
Unicameral People's Council
Judiciary High Court
Member of
CN, IMF, UN, UNESCO, WHO, WTO

LAND AND PEOPLE
Land area 115 sq mi (298 sq km)
Highest point 79 ft (24 m)
Coastline 400 mi (644 km)
Population 320,165
Major cities and populations
Malé 72,000
Ethnic groups
Sinhalese, Dravidian, Arab, African
Religion Islam
Languages
Divehi (official), Arabic, Hindi, English

ECONOMIC
Currency Rufiyaa
Industry
fish processing, tourism, coconut processing, garments, handicrafts
Agriculture
coconuts, corn, sweet potatoes
Natural resources
seafood

Mali

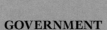

GOVERNMENT
Capital Bamako
Type of government Republic
Independence from France
August 22, 1960
Voting Universal adult suffrage
Head of state President
Head of government Prime
Minister
Constitution 1992
Legislature
Unicameral National Assembly
Judiciary Supreme Court
Member of
IMF, OAU UN, UNESCO, WHO,
WTO

LAND AND PEOPLE
Land area 478,839 sq mi
(1,240,192 sq km)
Highest point Hombori Tondo
3,789 ft (1,155 m)
Population 11,340,480
Major cities and populations
Bamako 800,000
Segou 106,000
Mopti 86,000
Ethnic groups
Mande 50%, Peul 17%, Voltaic 12%
Songhai 6%, Taureg/Moor 5%
Religions
Islam 90%, traditional animism 9%,
Christianity 1%
Languages
French (official), indigenous
languages

ECONOMIC
Currency CFA franc
Industry
food processing, mining
Agriculture
cotton, millet, rice, corn, vegetables,
peanuts, cattle, sheep, goats
Natural resources
gold, phosphates, kaolin, salt,
limestone, uranium, bauxite,
iron ore, manganese, tin, copper

Mali is a landlocked republic in northwestern Africa. It has the shape of two triangles linked together. Most of its land is low plain with some rocky hills. The northern third of the country lies in the Sahara Desert. The Hombori, Bambouk and Manding mountains rise in the south. The climate in the south is subtropical. Daytime temperatures often exceed 90°F. (32° C.) in the dry northern desert.

The largest ethnic group, the Mande, makes up about half the population. Other dominant groups are the Peul, Voltaic, Songhai, Tuareg and Moor. Nearly all of the people are Muslims. French is the official language. Many people speak Bambara or Songhai.

The region now known as Mali was part of the Ghana Empire until the eleventh century. The empire of Mali began at this time, reaching its peak in the fourteenth century. Its ruler, Mansa Musa, extended the empire to the Atlantic coast on the west and to Gao on the east. Mali was a major gold supplier from the early 1300s. Mali was gradually displaced by the Songhai Empire. Morocco invaded the area in 1591.

France gained control during the nineteenth century. It was named French Sudan in 1893. France made it a part of the Federation of French West Africa in the early 1900s.

Nationalist opposition, led by Modibo Keita, gathered strength between World Wars I and II. Mali became an autonomous state within the French Community in 1958. It was renamed the Sudanese Republic.

The Republic of Mali was declared on August 22, 1960. Keita was elected president. The country pursued socialist economic policies. President Keita dissolved the National Assembly in 1968. He was deposed in a military coup.

Military leader Moussa Traoré was elected president in the 1970s. His attempts to improve the economy were fruitless. A devastating drought caused more than 100,000 deaths, despite a major international aid effort. Another serious drought occurred in the 1980s. Traoré was removed in a 1991 coup.

Alpha Oumar Konaré was elected president in the first multi-party elections, held in 1992. Traoré and other military leaders were indicted for killings during the 1991 pro-democracy riots.

A rebellion by the Tuareg minority in northern Mali lasted through 1996. The I.M.F. and World Bank arranged major debt relief for Mali in 2000. The World Food Program delivered famine relief supplies. Konaré was reelected in 1997.

Malta

REPUBLIC OF MALTA

Malta comprises a group of islands in the central Mediterranean Sea. The largest is Malta, followed by Gozo, then Comino. The islands of Cominotto and Filfla are not inhabitable. Most of the landscape is low-lying with a rocky and indented coastline. Malta's climate features dry, hot summers and cool, wet winters.

More than ninety percent of the population is Maltese, a mix of several European cultures. Most of the population is Christian. English and Maltese are the official languages.

Malta uses about half of its land for farming. Some food must be imported due to poor soil. Malta manufactures a variety of consumer goods. Many people work in shipbuilding and repair. Tourism is increasingly vital to the economy.

People lived on Malta as early as 2000 B.C. Strategically located, it was successively occupied by Phoenicia, Greece, Carthage and Rome. Two centuries of Arab rule began in 870. Norman Crusaders occupied the islands in 1090 and annexed them to the kingdom of Sicily in 1127.

Holy Roman Emperor Charles V gave Malta to the Knights of Saint John of Jerusalem. They fought off an assault by the Ottoman Turks in 1565. The town of Valetta was established as a great fortress of the Mediterranean.

Napoleon of France expelled the knights in 1798, but British troops forced his withdrawal a year later. The terms of the Treaty of Paris made Malta a British crown colony in 1814.

Malta became a coaling station for steamships following the opening of the Suez Canal in 1869. Britain made it a major naval base.

Malta was given a constitution providing for its own legislature in 1921. It withstood repeated German and Italian air raids during World War II. Britain's King George VI awarded the colony, as a whole, the George Cross medal for heroism in 1942.

A constitution of 1961 gave Malta complete internal self-government. Nationalists won the first election. Independence was granted on September 21, 1963. Malta became a member of the U.N. in December. George Borg Olivier was the first prime minister.

Independence leader Dom Mintoff became president in 1971. Malta was declared a republic in 1974. The nation declared itself neutral and declined to renew an agreement for continued British military presence in 1979.

A vigorous program of economic reform and restructuring was begun in the 1990s and continues today. Malta has applied to join the European Union (EU).

GOVERNMENT
Website www.gov.mt
Capital Valetta
Type of government Republic
Independence from Britain
September 21, 1964
Voting Universal adult suffrage
Head of state President
Head of government Prime Minister
Constitution 1964, amended 1974
Legislature
Unicameral House of Representatives
Judiciary Constitutional Court
Member of
CN, IMF, UN, UNHCR, WHO, WTO

LAND AND PEOPLE
Land area 122 sq mi (316 sq km)
Highest point Dingli Cliffs
804 ft (245 m)
Coastline 157 mi (253 km)
Population 397,499
Major cities and populations
Birkirkara 24,000
Qormi 21,000
Hamrun 14,000
Valetta 9,500
Ethnic groups
Maltese 92%, others 8%
Religion Christianity
Languages
English, Maltese (both official)

ECONOMIC
Currency Maltese lira
Industry
tourism, electronics, shipbuilding and repair, food, beverages, textiles, footwear, clothing
Agriculture
potatoes, cauliflower, grapes, wheat, barley, tomatoes, citrus, cut flowers, peppers, pork, dairy, poultry
Natural resources
limestone, salt

Marshall Islands

REPUBLIC OF THE MARSHALL ISLANDS

Marshall Islands is an archipelago in the central Pacific Ocean between the Philippines and Hawaii. It is made up of five islands and 29 atolls spread out over 500,000 square miles (1,295,000 sq km) of ocean. The atolls include 1,200 islets. The weather is hot and humid throughout the year. Most of the rain falls between May and November. The country's 870 reef systems include about 160 species of coral and more than 800 species of fish.

Most Marshall Islanders are of Micronesian descent. They have a matriarchal society, which means that property rights are descended through women. Christianity is the majority religion, predominantly Protestant. English and Marshallese are the official languages. Japanese is also widely spoken.

Seafaring people from Southeast Asia are believed to have reached the islands in about 1000 B.C. The islands were sighted by the Spanish in A.D. 1526, but they were not colonized until centuries later. The islands were named after a British ship's captain who visited in 1788. Whaling and trading ships began making regular stops in the nineteenth century. The arrival of Christian missionaries caused great turmoil among the traditional tribal groups.

Germany made the Marshall Islands a protectorate, beginning in 1885. Japan seized the islands during World War I. The League of Nations mandated them to Japan in 1920. The islands saw some major battles between Allied and Japanese forces during World War II. They came under United States control beginning in 1944.

The United States used the Bikini and Enewetak atolls shalls for nuclear weapons testing from 1946 to 1958. Resulting health problems have been addressed in recent years. Enewetak was re-inhabited in the 1970s. Bikini was declared safe for habitation in 1996.

The Marshall Islands were made a trusteeship of the U.S. in 1947. They became self-governing in 1979, in free association with the United States. The United States took control of Marshallese defense and foreign affairs, and retained its military bases there. The trusteeship was dissolved in 1990, although the islands continue to receive U. S. aid. The Marshall Islands joined the U.N. in 1991.

Amata Nabua served as president of the Marshall Islands from 1979 until his death in 1996. He was succeeded by Imata Kabua. Weather patterns associated with El Nino caused a severe drought during 1997 and 1998. Kessai Note was elected president in 2001.

Mauritania

ISLAMIC REPUBLIC OF MAURITANIA

All of Mauritania lies within the Sahara Desert, except for a narrow fertile strip in the south. Mauritania is bounded by Algeria, Mali and Senegal in northwestern Africa. Daytime inland temperatures exceed 100° F. (37.8°C.) for more than half the year. Rainfall is erratic and minimal. The coastal climate is more tropical than that of the inland areas.

The majority of the people are "black" Moors of Sudanic origin. Most of these people have settled in the fertile area near the Senegal River. Some of the "white" Moors, of mixed Arab and Berber backgrounds, are still nomads. Almost all Mauritanians are Sunni Muslims. Arabic is the official language.

There is evidence of human civilizations in the northern Saharan regions during the Stone Age. Berber migrants pushed the original Soninke inhabitants south in the third century A.D. Mauritania formed the core of the Ghana Empire between the seventh and eleventh centuries.

Ghana was overrun by the Islamic state of Almoravid during the eleventh and twelfth centuries. The Mali Kingdom then became dominant. Invasions by Bedouin Arabs were met by fierce Berber resistance until the Arabs conquered the area in the sixteenth century.

Islam was introduced during this time.

Portugal established trading posts on the coast in the 1400s. France gained control of the region under the 1814 Treaty of Paris. It became part of French West Africa, with indigenous rulers, in 1903. Mauritania became a full colony in 1920. It was named an overseas territory of the French Union in 1946.

The Islamic Republic of Mauritania within the French Community was proclaimed in 1958. Two years later, on November 28, 1960, it became fully independent. President Moktar Ould Daddah established one-party rule the following year. He was reelected four times in the years to follow.

Mauritania suffered from severe drought in the 1960s and early 1970s. Its economy expanded as newly discovered iron and copper deposits were exploited. A series of military coups and abrupt changes in leadership occurred from the late 1970s through the early 1990s.

The first elections with full participation by opposition parties were held in 1994. Maouya Ould Sidi Ahmed Taya was elected president. The economy has continued to improve. The Arabization of Mauritanian society continues to cause friction with its African peoples. Taya was reelected in 2001.

GOVERNMENT
Website www.mauritania.mr
Capital Nouakchott
Type of government
Republic
Independence from France
November 28, 1960
Voting Universal adult suffrage
Head of state President
Head of government Prime Minister
Constitution 1991
Legislature
Bicameral Parliament
National Assembly (lower house),
Senate (upper house)
Judiciary Supreme Court
Member of AL, IMF, OAU, UN,
UNESCO, WHO, WTO

LAND AND PEOPLE
Land area 398,000 sq mi
(1,030,700 sq km)
Highest point Kediet Ijill
2,986 ft (910 m)
Coastline 469 mi (754 km)
Population 2,828,850
Major cities and populations
Nouakchott 750,000
Nouadhibou 75,000
Ethnic groups
Arab-Berber, Haratin, Tukolor,
Fulani, Wolof, Soninke
Religion
Islam 99%
Languages
Arabic (official), French, Poular,
Wolof, Soninke

ECONOMIC
Currency Ouguiya
Industry seafood processing,
mining
Agriculture dates, millet,
sorghum, rice, corn, cattle, sheep
Natural resources
iron ore, gypsum, copper,
phosphate, diamonds, gold, oil,
seafood

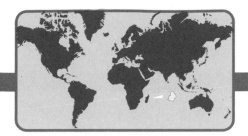

Mauritius

REPUBLIC OF MAURITIUS

Mauritius is a group of islands located east of Madagascar in the Indian Ocean. The country includes the islands of Mauritius, Rodrigues and Agalega, as well as the Saint Brandon Group of 22 small islands. The main island of Mauritius was formed by an ancient volcano. A low-lying plain in the north rises to a central plateau which covers much of the island. From this plateau the mountains of the south rise. The island is almost entirely surrounded by coral reefs. The subtropical climate is consistently warm and humid.

Around two-thirds of the population is of Indian descent. Hinduism is the dominant religion, while Christianity and Islam account for significant percentages. English is the official language. French Creole is spoken by many people.

Mauritius became a regular stopping off point for Arab and Malay voyagers before the fifteenth century. The first European visitors were Portuguese. The Dutch established a settlement named after Prince Maurice of Nassau in 1598. They imported slaves to aid in harvesting the island's ebony trees until 1710.

The French claimed Mauritius, renaming it Île de France in 1715. The Compagnie des Indes established sugar plantations which also used slave labor. The British conquered Mauritius in 1810, reinstating the previous name. Britain abolished slavery in the 1830s. Plantation owners imported indentured laborers from India.

Descendants of the original French settlers held political power until 1947. Then an expansion of voting rights shifted the balance of power to the Indian population. Independence from Britain came on March 12, 1968. The British monarch was head of state and Seewoosagur Ramgoolan was prime minister.

Mauritius enjoyed an economic boom until sugar prices dropped in the late 1970s. Ramgoolan was replaced by Aneerood Jugnauth in 1982. Mauritius became a republic on March 12, 1992. Cassem Uteem was elected president.

Mauritius continues a dispute with Britain over ownership of the nearby Chagos Archipelago. Ramgoolan's son Navin became prime minister in 1995. Jugnauth regained the office after the elections of 2000. President Cassem Uteem resigned in 2002. He opposed antiterrorist measures which threatened human rights. When faced with the legislature's antiterrorist bill, he explained that he would prefer to resign rather than sign the legislation into law. Prime Minister Jugnauth supports the legislation.

Mexico

UNITED MEXICAN STATES

Mexico occupies the southernmost portion of the North American continent, sharing a long land border with the United States in the north. The landscape is dominated by an immense central plateau running north to south. The Sierra Madre Oriental range dominates the east, the Sierra Madre Occidental the west. Most of the north is desert. There are wide coastal plains on the Caribbean Sea and Pacific Ocean coastlines. The climate varies according to the elevation. The coastal lowlands are most often hot and humid. The high country is usually cold. Rainfall varies considerably throughout the country.

The large majority of Mexicans are Mestizos, people whose ancestors were indigenous and Spanish. Some thirty percent have indigenous backgrounds and just under ten percent are of European descent. Mexico is predominantly Christian, with Catholicism accounting for nearly ninety percent of the population. Most people speak Spanish, the official language. More than fifty dialects are used by indigenous groups.

The strength of the Mexican economy has varied dramatically in recent years. Traditionally many indstries have been controlled by the government. A privatization program begun in the early 1990s slowed when the Mexican currency collapsed in 1995. Tough austerity measures and strong export earnings have since aided the economy.

Agriculture is important to the Mexican economy. Irrigation is essential in nearly all areas. Mexico's principal crops are cotton, coffee, sugar cane, citrus fruits, tomatoes and wheat. Livestock includes cattle, hogs, goats, sheep, horses, mules and chickens. Fishing is also a key industry.

Mexico's most valuable mineral resource is oil. Silver, copper, gold and iron are also mined throughout the country.

Industrial growth has centered on the maquiladoras since the 1980s. These are assembly factories located in regional areas. They use low-cost labor to assemble products from parts made elsewhere. Manufactured products includes machinery, electronic equipment, chemicals, food and drink, textiles, motor vehicles, glass and pottery.

The huge Mayan temple at Chichen Itza.

BRAND X PICTURES

Mexico is a federal republic of thirty-one states under a constitution adopted in 1917. The president is head of state and head of government. The president is elected directly by the people and can serve only one six-year term. A cabinet is appointed by the president. The bicameral legislature is made up of the Chamber of Deputies and the Senate. Deputies are elected for three years. Senators hold office for six years. Legislators may not serve two consecutive terms.

Mexico was the site of a number of great civilizations. The earliest was the Olmec, which flourished between 1500 and 600 B.C. The Mayan civilization came next, reaching its peak in the sixth century A.D. The Toltec migrated from the north. In the tenth century they established an empire, founding the cities of Tula and Tulancingo. The Toltec civilization ended in the twelfth century. The Aztecs founded an empire based at Tenochtitlan. These people prevailed until the Spanish conquest in 1521. Great heights of learning and culture were achieved under these civilizations.

Spanish conquistadors, led by Hernando Cortés, landed in what is now Mexico in 1519. They were vast in number and used superior weaponry. The conquistadors defeated the Aztecs and captured their leader Moctezuma II. Two years later they overran the Aztec capital.

Aztec culture was of little interest to Spaniards concerned only with finding gold and silver. The region became the viceroyalty of New Spain in 1535. The Catholic Church soon developed a strong hold on the region.

The indigenous people were forced to work for their colonizers. The Spanish made attempts to improve conditions for the workers on farms and mines, but to no avail. Silver deposits discovered at Zacatecas in 1546 made New Spain a key part of the Spanish empire.

The colony was expanded north and south, but little was done to improve living conditions for the people. Manufacturing was banned. Silver and gold were shipped to Spain.

A rigid class structure evolved with Spaniards born in Spain on the top. Next came the Spaniards born in Mexico. Mestizos, those of mixed Spanish and indigenous blood were third and indigenous peoples were at the bottom.

Change began in the early nineteenth century when Spain was conquered by Napoleon's forces in 1808. A Mexican independence movement was established, led by Fr. Miguel Hidalgo y Costilla. He issued his document demanding independence on September 16, 1810. He was executed the fol-

Mexico

BRAND X PICTURES

Parts of Mexico, such as Xcaret Beach, are especially inviting to tourists.

They were determined to protect their privileged positions, so they supported the Mexican Empire of Augustin de Iturbide in 1822. The empire collapsed after just ten months. A republic was proclaimed with Guadelupe Victoria as president. Spanish military forces failed in a 1829 attempt to regain control.

At this time, Mexico included large areas of what is now the United States. Texas' independence declaration in 1836 led to war with Mexico. This escalated into a wider conflict with the United States from 1846 to 1848. It ended with the Treaty of Guadelupe Hidalgo under which Mexico surrendered California, New Mexico, Arizona, Nevada, part of Colorado and Utah to the United States. In return it was paid U.S.$15 million and its debts were cancelled.

Corruption and unstable governments prevailed in the mid-nineteenth century. The most prominent president during this time was military leader Antonio López de Santa Anna, who served 1832–36 and 1841–44. He regained power after the war with the United States. Santa Anna became a dictator-president until 1855 when he was overthrown by revolutionaries led by liberal Benito Juárez.

The new constitution of 1857 greatly reduced the property holdings of the Catholic Church and trimmed privileges for the military. Conservatives reacted angrily, sparking a war which raged from 1858 to 1861.

Juárez suspended payment of foreign debts because of economic pressure. Britain, France and Spain jointly invaded Mexico as a result. Napoleon III's forces entered Mexico City in 1863. The Habsburg Archduke Ferdinand Maximilian was created Emperor of Mexico. The French withdrew four years later. Juárez regained power.

Porfirio Díaz became president after an armed revolt in 1877. He embarked on a program of economic reconstruction, building industries, railroads, public works and harbors. This was financed by foreign investors. Mexico had regained its international credit standing by the beginning of the twentieth century. Díaz retained power until 1911, except for one period from 1880 to 1884. He led a regime which entrenched the power of the wealthy minority.

The Mexican Revolution began in 1910 as a revolt against the policies of Diaz. Rebel leader Francisco Madero became very popular with the people. Francisco "Pancho" Villa began a war in the north while Emilian Zapata led a peasants' revolt in the south.

lowing year. When a liberal revolution swept Spain in 1821, the independence movement deposed the Spanish viceroy.

The conservative Mexican elite feared these changes.

Heavy traffic congestion is a part of everyday life in Mexico City.

FLAT EARTH PICTURE GALLERY

Diaz was forced to resign in 1911. Francisco Madero was elected president. Victoriano Huerta, head of Madero's army, conspired against the president. Huerta became dictator in 1913. He had Madera murdered.

New revolts began under Zapata, Villa and Venustiano Carranza. Huerta resigned in 1914. Carranza took power the same year. A commission of eight Latin American countries and the U. S. recognized Carranza as the lawful authority in Mexico. The rebel leaders, with the exception of Villa, ended the fighting. About 250,000 people had died in the war.

BRAND X PICTURES

Vegetables on sale at Playa del Carmen.

The new constitution of 1917 brought major changes in labor and social welfare programs. Communal lands were returned to indigeous people. Restrictions were placed on the power of the Catholic Church.

The presidency of General Lázaro Cárdenas, from 1934 to 1949, was marked by a number of radical actions. He encouraged labor unions and introduced additional land reforms. The railway system and the oil industry were nationalized. Control was taken from foreign companies.

Mexican support for the Allies led to substantial aid from the United States during World War II. This laid a basis for decades of economic development. Vast irrigation projects began and transportation was upgraded. Mexico also benefited from a growth in the number of American tourists.

Economic growth slowed in the 1970s. Repayment of large international loans became a substantial burden following a drop in the price of oil. President Miguel de la Madrid Hurtado, elected in 1982, imposed strict economic controls. The crisis only deepened when Mexico City was rocked by an earthquake which killed 9,500 people in 1985.

Privatization of state enterprises began under President Carlos Salinas de Gortari in the

Mexico

early 1990s. Relations with the United States were strained by the continuing flow of illegal immigrants heading north seeking work. Narcotics trafficking was also a problem.

Mexico's economic position was enhanced when it joined with the United States and Canada to form the North American Free Trade Agreement (NAFTA) in 1992. This removed many trade barriers and tariffs, giving Mexico access to a market of more than 370 million people.

The dire poverty of the indigenous people provoked an uprising in 1994. Zapatista rebels took over towns in Chiapas, a state in the south. Dozens of people died before the government promised another wave of reforms.

Mexico's economy collapsed under the weight of crippling foreign debt and the withdrawal of foreign investment in 1994. A large section of the petrochemical industry was privatized and economic controls tightened. These measures were demanded by the International Monetary Fund (IMF) and the United States in return for financial support. The currency was devalued, increasing the prices of most products. Unemployment grew steadily.

The presidential election of 2000 was a major turning point in Mexican politics. The Institutional Revolutionary Party had ruled Mexico since the 1930s. Its presidential candidate was defeated by Vincente Fox Quesada of the National Action Party in July of 2000.

It was announced in 2000 that debts resulting from the mid-1990s economic crisis had been paid. Problems with the Zapatista rebels in Chiapas continue to cause friction in Mexican society despite Fox's efforts to institute change.

The Cathedral Merida at Yucatan.

Micronesia

FEDERATED STATES OF MICRONESIA

Micronesia is located between the Philippines and Hawaii in the Pacific Ocean. It is made up of four main groups of islands, Pohnpei, Chuuk, Yap and Kosrae. It includes more than 600 islands and islets. The island of Pohnpei accounts for nearly half the country's total land area. The climate is tropical, with high temperatures, humidity and abundant rainfall all year round.

Most of the population is Micronesian, descended from the original arrivals about 3000 years ago. Christianity is the religion of the majority. English is the official language. Eight Polynesian languages are spoken in various places.

Polynesian peoples from other parts of the Pacific settled on the islands around 1000 B.C. The first Europeans to sight them were the Spaniards in A.D. 1565. Few Europeans visited the islands, generally known as the Carolines, until the nineteenth century. Then an influx of traders and missionaries introduced infectious diseases which killed large numbers of islanders.

The Carolines were formally annexed by Spain in 1874. Twenty-five years later they were sold to Germany following the Spanish–American War. Little development occurred.

Japanese forces removed the German administrators and occupied the islands when World War I began in 1914. The League of Nations granted Japan a mandate over the Carolines in 1920.

The Chuuk Lagoon was developed as a Japanese naval base. It played a key part in Japan's military strategy during World War II. The lagoon was heavily bombarded by the U. S. Along with neighboring island groups, the Carolines became a United Nations Trust Territory under United States administration in 1947.

The residents of the primary islands voted to confederate. The Federated States of Micronesia was formed in 1979. Micronesia entered a compact of free association with the United States. This agreement provided for full self-government with the U. S. taking responsibility for defense.

The trusteeship was formally dissolved by the U.N. Security Council in 1990. Micronesia was admitted to the U.N. the following year.

Micronesia spent most of the 1990s struggling to improve its economy. The compact of free association with the U. S. expired in 2001. The U. S. and Micronesia have signed a new compact of financial aid which will eventually provide full-self-sufficiency to the country. This compact is pending the approval of the U. S. Congress by fall of 2003.

Moldova

REPUBLIC OF MOLDOVA

Moldova is located in southeastern Europe between Romania and Ukraine. The land is primarily a hilly plain. Numerous deep valleys and gorges are crossed by many rivers including the Prut and the Dnestr. The climate is mild to warm.

Sixty-five percent of the people is Moldovan. Most of the remainder are either Russian or Ukrainian. Most people of Moldova follow either the Eastern Orthodox or the Russian Orthodox Church. Moldavian is the official language.

The area of present-day Moldova was once part of the ancient Roman province of Daca. It was ruled by the Kievan Rus and then the Tatars in centuries that followed. It became an independent principality of Romania known as Moldavia by the fourteenth century. The Turkish Ottoman Empire took control in the sixteenth century.

The east of Moldavia was conquered by Russia in 1791. Romania annexed the south in 1856, during the Crimean War.

The remainder passed from the Ottomans to the Romanians by 1918. Although it was confirmed by the 1920 Treaty of Paris, the Soviet Union refused to accept the arrangement. It established the Moldavian Autonomous Soviet Socialist Republic in 1924.

The Nazi–Soviet pact of 1940 forced Romania to surrender most of Moldavia to the Soviet Union. Cross-migration was encouraged, with Ukrainians and Russians settling in Moldavia, and Moldavians moving elsewhere. The country was occupied by Romania during World War II.

Demands for the restoration of the Moldavian language and cessation of migration prompted large demonstrations by the Popular Front of Moldavia in the late 1980s. Political reforms began as the USSR neared its end. Several groups declared ethnically based republics within Moldavia.

The Republic of Moldova was formed as the USSR collapsed in 1991. Moldova was the Romanian name for the region. Full independence came on August 27. Moldova joined the Commonwealth of Independent States (CIS) shortly thereafter. A referendum in 1994 demonstrated overwhelming support for continued independence rather than unification with Romania.

The heavily Russian and Ukrainian Trans-Dnestr region fought for independence through 1997 when a peace accord was signed. The Communist Party won a majority in parliament in the 2001 elections. Its leader, Vladimir Voronin, was elected president.

GOVERNMENT
Website www.moldova.md
Capital Chisinau
Type of government Republic
Separation from Soviet Union August 27, 1991
Voting Universal adult suffrage
Head of state President
Head of government Prime Minister
Constitution 1991
Legislature Unicameral Parliament
Judiciary Supreme Court
Member of CE, IMF, OECD, UN, UNESCO, WHO, WTO

LAND AND PEOPLE
Land area 13,000 sq mi (33,700 sq km)
Highest point Dealul Balaneshty 1,410 ft (430 m)
Population 4,434,547
Major cities and populations Chisinau 750,000
Ethnic groups Moldovan 65%, Ukranian 14%, Russian 13%, others 8%
Religions Christianity
Languages Moldavian (official)

ECONOMIC
Currency Moldovan leu
Industry food processing, agricultural machinery, electrical appliances, sugar refining, vegetable oil, footwear, textiles
Agriculture vegetables, fruits, wine, grain, beet sugar, sunflower seed, beef, dairy
Natural resources lignite, phosphorites, gypsum, limestone

Monaco

PRINCIPALITY OF MONACO

Monaco is a small independent state in southwestern Europe, occupying only .75 square miles (1.95 sq km). It is an enclave in southeastern France, where its hilly landscape borders the Mediterranean Sea. The climate features hot, dry summers. Most of its rain falls during the cool winters.

Half of Monaco's people are of French origin, some sixteen percent are Monégasque (born in Monaco), and there is a similar number of Italians. Almost all are Roman Catholic. French is the official language, but Monégasque, a French Provençal–Italian hybrid, is also spoken.

Tourism is the foundation of the economy of Monaco. The sale of postage stamps and tobacco, banking and insurance, and the manufacture of pharmaceuticals, electronic equipment, cosmetics, and plastic goods are also important. Gambling is another large source of income.

The name Monaco derives from the Ligurian Monoikos tribe which dwelt in the area during the sixth century B.C. The Phoenicians, Greeks, Romans, Visigoths and Saracens occupied the area during the next several centuries.

The Grimaldi family of Genoa, Italy, acquired the territory in 1297. They developed a strong alliance with France and became established at Monaco in 1489.

Napoleon of France annexed Monaco during the French Revolution in 1793. Monaco was made a protectorate of Sardinia by the terms of the Treaty of Vienna in 1815. It was restored as an independent state under the guardianship of France in 1861. Prince Albert I granted it a constitution in 1911.

Monaco developed as an elite tourist center after World War II. Its gambling casino was a principal attraction. World attention was focused on Prince Rainier III's 1956 marriage to American actress Grace Kelly.

Greek shipping tycoon Aristotle Onassis bought up much of Monaco's commercial interests during the 1950s. Friction developed between Onassis and the Grimaldis. The principality purchased his interests in 1967.

Monaco's status as a tax haven causes friction with other European countries. Recent accusations of serious financial improprieties have been made by the French parliament. Monaco has threatened to sever relations with France.

Princess Grace died in September of 1982 following a automobile accident. Prince Albert, heir to throne, is becoming more involved in the government as his father, the reigning monarch Prince Rainier III, deals with health problems.

Mongolia

Mongolia is a landlocked republic in northern central Asia. Much of the country is a plateau broken by mountain ranges in the north and west, the largest of which are the majestic Altai Mountains. The vast Gobi Desert in central and southeast Mongolia covers one-third of the country. Winters are long, with sub-zero temperatures. Summers can be mild to warm in places.

The Khalkha Mongol make up ninety percent of the population. There is a small Kazakh population in the west. Other minorities include Russians and Chinese. Tibetan Buddhism prevailed until it was banned by the communists in the 1930s. A slow resurgence began in the 1990s. The Kazakhs are Muslims. Most Mongolians speak Khalka Mongol.

Mongolia was inhabited by nomadic tribal groups before 1000 B.C. They began forming large empires during the third century B.C. Genghis Khan created the first Mongol state in A.D. 1206. He began a campaign of territorial expansion. Mongol armies pressed as far as eastern Europe.

Mongol control of China collapsed in the fourteenth century. China's Manchu dynasty occupied Mongolia in the 1690s. Mongolia declared its independence from China after the Chinese Revolution of 1911.

A military force supplied by Japan and led by Russian anti-Bolsheviks took Urga, the capital city, in 1920. The Mongolian People's Republic army, trained by Soviets and aided by the USSR, defeated the anti-Bolsheviks the following year.

The Communist Mongolian People's Republic was founded in 1924. Landowners were stripped of property and agriculture was collectivized. Buddhist leaders were persecuted. Large numbers of Mongolians fled to China.

Japan's 1939 invasion was repelled by Mongolian and Soviet troops. Mongolia developed close ties with the USSR, which sponsored its 1961 admission to the U.N. The two nations signed a treaty of mutual assistance.

Widespread demonstrations led to multi-party elections in 1990. A new constitution was written liberalizing the government. The elections of 1996 brought the new Democratic Union coalition to power. It was the first non-communist government in seventy years. Econonic reforms were begun.

Soviet aid had accounted for one-third of Mongolia's budget. Mongolia has instituted more liberal policies and opened up industry to foreign investment. Its economic growth into the 2000s has been slow. The former Communists returned to power in the 2000 elections.

GOVERNMENT
Website www.pmis.gov.mn
Capital Ulaan Baatar
Type of government Republic
Independence from China
July 11, 1921
Voting Universal adult suffrage
Head of state President
Head of government Prime
Minister
Constitution 1992
Legislature
Unicameral State Great Hural
Judiciary Supreme Court
Member of
IMF, UN, UNESCO, WHO, WTO

LAND AND PEOPLE
Land area 604,250 sq mi
(1,565,000 sq km)
Highest point
Taran Bogd Uul
14,350 ft (4,374 m)
Population 2,694,432
Major cities and populations
Ulan Bator 668,000
Darhan 75,000
Erdenet 71,000
Ethnic groups
Khalka Mongol 90%, Kazakh 3%,
Russian 2%, Chinese 2%, other 3%
Religions Buddhism, Islam
Languages Khalkha Mongol

ECONOMIC
Currency Tugrik
Industry
construction materials, mining, oil,
food, beverages, animal products
Agriculture
wheat, barley, potatoes, sheep,
goats, cattle, camels, horses
Natural resources
oil, coal, copper, molybdenum,
tungsten, phosphates, tin, nickel,
zinc, wolfram, fluorspar, gold, silver,
iron, phosphate

Morocco

KINGDOM OF MOROCCO

GOVERNMENT
Website www.mincom.gov.ma
Capital Rabat
Type of government
Constitutional monarchy
Independence from France
March 2, 1956
Voting Universal adult suffrage
Head of state Monarch
Head of government Prime
Minister
Constitution 1972
Legislature
Bicameral Parliament
Chamber of Representatives (lower
house), Chamber of Counsellors
(upper house)
Judiciary Supreme Court
Member of AL, IMF, UN, UNESCO,
UNHCR, WHO, WTO

LAND AND PEOPLE
Land area 172,414 sq mi
(446,550 sq km)
Highest point Jebel Toubkal
13,665 ft (4,165 m)
Coastline 1,149 mi (1,835 km)
Population 31,167,783
Major cities and populations
Casablanca 3.1 million
Marrakesh 1.5 million
Rabat 1.4 million
Ethnic groups
Arab-Berber 99%
Religions Muslim 99%, others 1%
Languages
Arabic (official), indigenous
languages

ECONOMIC
Currency Moroccan dirham
Industry
mining, food processing,
leather goods, textiles, tourism
Agriculture
barley, wheat, citrus, wine,
vegetables, olives, livestock
Natural resources
phosphates, iron ore, manganese,
lead, zinc, seafood, salt

Located in northwest Africa, Morocco has coastlines on both the Mediterranean Sea and Atlantic Ocean. It has the broadest plains and highest mountains in Africa. Highlands called the Er Rif parallel the Mediterranean. The Atlas Mountains extend across the country from the Er Rif to the Atlantic. Broad coastal plains run along the Atlantic Ocean. Plains south of the Atlas Mountains merge with the Sahara Desert in the southeast. The climate is arid in the Sahara and temperate on the coasts.

The population is a mix of Arab and Berber ancestry. Islam is the state religion. Nearly all Moroccans are Sunni Muslims. Arabic is Morocco's official language. A number of Berber dialects are also spoken.

Berber tribes have inhabited the region since about 1500 B.C. The Phoenicians established trading posts on the Mediterranean coast in the twelfth century B.C. These areas were later seized and expanded by the Carthaginians. Rome conquered the area in the second century B.C. It was made part of the Roman Empire in A.D.42. Christianity was introduced during this time. Vandals and Byzantines ruled from 429 through the 600s. Arabs arrived in 682, bringing Islam and all but eliminating Christianity.

Arab King Idris I founded a dynasty which lasted from 788 to 926. Inter-tribal warfare led to many changes during the next century. The Almoravids ruled from 1062 to 1147, followed by the Almohads until 1258. Morocco built an empire that included modern-day Algeria, Tunisia, Libya and parts of Spain and Portugal.

The reign of the Saadians began what is known as the golden age of Morroco in 1554. Millions of Jews and Moors

The Hassan II mosque dominates the skyline of Casablanca.

FLAT EARTH PICTURE GALLERY

47

Morocco

arrived from Spain. Art and architecture flourished.

Portugal and Spain began colonizing coastal areas of Morocco as early as the fifteenth century. Morocco regained control of these areas by the end of the seventeenth century. The countries of Europe were concerned about the future of Morroco because of its crucial position on the Mediterranean Sea. France and Spain agreed to divide and take possession of Morocco in 1904.

The French gradually annexed most of the country, claiming they were controlling the warring factions. Tangier remained an international zone and Spain held about ten percent of the country. Sultan Abd al-Hafiz signed a treaty making his country a French protectorate in 1912. He needed European support to maintain order.

Fighting continued between Berber guerrillas and Spanish and French forces until 1934. The Vichy government of France allowed Morocco to support the Germans in World War II. Allied forces invaded in November 1942, crushing all opposition within days.

Sultan Muhammed V ben Youssef began an independence movement in the mid-1940s. The French exiled him in 1953. Two years later, after a major revolt in Morocco, they permitted him to

A medieval fort in the harbor at Essaouria.

return. Morocco became an independent sultanate on March 2, 1956. Spain maintained control of some small areas.

The sultan was named King Mohammed V in 1957. A much-delayed constitution was adopted in 1962. Mohamed's successor, his son Hassan II, declared a state of emergency and suspended the legislature in 1965. He tightened his control on the nation in the early 1970s, having survived several assassination attempts.

Hassan claimed Spanish Sahara as Moroccan territory in 1974. He was opposed by the Polisario Front, which sought independence for the region. U.N. negotiators made unsuccessful attempts to resolve the situation.

Morocco sent troops to protect Saudi Arabia when Iraq

invaded Kuwait in 1990. It had no direct role in the Persian Gulf War.

Hassan died in 1999. He was replaced by his son Muhammed VI. The new king made himself popular by freeing large numbers of political prisoners. He also declared his support for women's equality. The question of Spanish Sahara remains undecided. The United Nations continues to press for a much-delayed referendum to settle the 28-year conflict.

Five suicide bombers killed 24 and wounded 60 in Casablanca in May of 2003. Most victims were Jewish or Spanish. The attacks are believed to be the work of the al-Qaeda terrorist network. Many suspected members of the al-Qaeda terrorist network were arrested in 2002.

Mozambique

REPUBLIC OF MOZAMBIQUE

Mozambique is a republic in southeastern Africa. It is crossed by numerous large rivers, including the Zambezi. Coastal lowlands give way to plateaus and mountains in the west and the north. The northwestern plateau abuts the western border of the Great Rift Valley. Much of the southern coastline is mangrove swamps. The climate is tropical with a rainy season from December to March.

The Makua people of the northern areas make up about half the population. The Tsonga people are dominant in the south. About half the people follow traditional animist beliefs. Thirty percent are Christians, while most of the remainder are Muslims. Portuguese is the official language. Bantu and Swahili dialects are widely spoken.

The San people were overcome by Bantu-speaking immigrants in the fourth century. Arab gold and ivory traders began establishing city-states in the late eighth century.

Portugese traders built coastal settlements following the arrival of explorer Vasco da Gama in 1498. Their exploration of inland areas disrupted native farms, but they found little wealth. Slave trading became widespread by the seventeenth century. Portuguese missionaries converted many to Christianity. Farmland was offered to Europeans.

Mozambique became a Portuguese overseas province in 1951. The Front for the Liberation of Mozambique (Frelimo) launched a guerrilla war against Portugal in 1962. Its leader was assassinated by the Portuguese in 1969.

A 1974 coup in Portugal brought to power a government that withdrew from Mozambique. The country became independent on June 25, 1975. Samora Machel was president. He began nationalizing the country's industries and creating farming collectives. About 250,000 Portugese fled the country. These people made up much of the technical and professional class. Their departure seriously harmed the economy.

Mozambique aided guerrillas fighting the white regime in Rhodesia. Rhodesia funded the Mozambique National Resistance (Renamo) in an attempt to topple the Mozambique government. South Africa took over Renamo's funding in the 1980s. Civil war ensued, followed by a great famine. More than 900,000 people died by 1990, while another 1.3 million people fled the country.

Joaquim Chissano won the 1999 presidential election amid claims of electoral fraud. Record floods in the south killed 600, displaced a million others, and seriously damaged the country's economy in early 2000. Mozambique remains one of the world's poorest countries.

Myanmar

UNION OF MYANMAR

Myanmar is located in Southeast Asia. A horseshoe-shaped mountain complex and the Irrawaddy River basin and delta make up much of the country. The Arakan Yoma Mountains create a natural border with India on the west, while the Bilauktaung Range lies near the boundary of southeastern Myanmar and Thailand. The northeast is dominated by the Shan Plateau, which originates in China. It has an equatorial climate, with a slight cooling from November to February.

Seventy percent of the population is of Burman descent. The Karen and Shan people make up significant minorities. Almost all of the people are Theravada Buddhists. Burmese is the official language. Over 100 indigenous languages are also in use.

Various groups of people traveled down the Irrawaddy River from China and Tibet to Myanmar. They were influenced by social and political institutions carried across the sea from India. The Mon were the first to arrive, perhaps as early as 3000 B.C. They built settlements and developed trade with India. The Mon were joined by the Pyu in the first century B.C. Both groups were absorbed by the Burmans in the ninth century A.D.

The Burman King Anawratha began his control over much of the south in 1044. He established the Pagan dynasty in 1057, unifying all of the country. The Mongol armies of Kublai Khan brought an end to the dynasty in 1287.

The Shan people dominated the north, while the Mons controlled the south. The Toungood dynasty of the sixteenth century reunited the state. A Mons revolution toppled the dynasty in 1752. King Alaungpaya founded the Konbaung dynasty shortly thereafter. He gradually returned the area to Burman control and expanded the country beyond its former borders.

Britain's determination to block the Konbaung's westward expansion sparked the first Anglo–Burmese war in 1824. Britain gained possession of the Irrawaddy delta region after the second war in 1852. The country became a province of British India in 1885, after a third war.

Rice growing was greatly expanded and railways were constructed under Britain's control. The country, then known as Burma, gained internal self-government by 1937.

Japan conquered Burma in 1942, establishing the Burma Independence Army (BIA) to fight the Allies. The Anti-Fascist People's Freedom League (AFPFL), led by U Aung San, conducted a guerrilla war against the Japanese and campaigned for independence.

Buddhist monks collecting alms.

U Aung San and six of his cabinet were assassinated in 1947. The Union of Burma became independent on January 4, 1948. Prime Minister U Nu's government came under attack from communist-backed insurgents. The Karen people and other groups struggled for independence. Most rebellions were suppressed by 1951. Ethnic regions were granted some autonomy.

After the AFPFL split into two factions in 1958, General Ne Win took control until elections were held. U Nu was restored to the leadership. He renewed ethnic strife by making Buddhism the state religion.

An army coup d'état in March 1962 returned Ne Win to power. The constitution was suspended and the Revolutionary Council ruled by decree. People were reorganized into workers' and peasants' councils and a one-party state was established. All industry was nationalized. Chinese-backed rebels increased internal strife. They eventually controlled much of the country.

A new constitution with a unicameral legislature was created in March 1974. Widespread anti-government rioting forced Ne Win to resign the presidency in 1988. The army once more took control in 1989 as the State Law and Order Committee (SLORC). A brutal crackdown

on dissenters followed. Burma was renamed Myanmar, to better represent the various ethnic groups.

Elections in May 1990 gave a sweeping victory to the National League for Democracy (NLD). It was led by Daw Aung San Suu Kyi, daughter of the independence leader U Aung San. SLORC refused to accept the result, imprisoning NLD members and placing Suu Kyi under house arrest. She was awarded the Nobel Peace Prize in 1991.

General Than Shwe took over as national leader the following year. Martial law was eased and political prisoners released. Rebel movements were calmed. Daw Aung San Suu Kyi was released in 1995.

Widespread reports of the regime's involvement in drug trade and forced labor practices appeared during the 1990s. The regime was renamed the State Peace and Development Council (SPDC) in 1997. It began talks of encouraging international investment.

Myanmar was admitted to membership of the Association of South-East Asian Nations (ASEAN) in 1999. Suu Kyi was once more arrested in September 2000. She has been quoted as saying she believes her 2002 release was an indication of positive changes for Myanmar.

GOVERNMENT
Website www.myanmar.com
Capital Yangon
Type of government
Military dictatorship
Independence from Britain
January 4,, 1948
Voting Universal adult suffrage
Head of state and government
Prime Minister and Chairman of the State Peace and Development Council
Constitution
1974, suspended 1988
Legislature
Unicameral People's Assembly (Pyithu Hluttaw), unconvened since 1990
Judiciary undefined
Member of ASEAN, IMF, UN, UNESCO, WHO, WTO

LAND AND PEOPLE
Land area 261,217 sq mi
(676,552 sq km)
Highest point Hkakabo Razi
19,284 ft (5,881 m)
Coastline 1,199 mi (1,930 km)
Population 48,238,224
Major cities and populations
Yangon 3,500,000
Mandalay 850,000
Ethnic groups Burman 70%, Shan 9%, Karen 7%, others 14%
Religions Buddhism 89%, Christianity 4%, Islam 4%
Languages
Burmese (official), indigenous languages

ECONOMIC
Currency Kyat
Industry
agricultural processing, mining, clothing, wood products, copper, tin, tungsten, iron, construction materials pharmaceuticals, fertilizer
Agriculture
rice, beans, sesame, nuts, sugar cane, timber
Natural resources
petroleum, timber, tin, antimony, zinc, copper, tungsten, lead, coal, limestone, precious stones, natural gas

Namibia

REPUBLIC OF NAMIBIA

Namibia is a country in southwestern Africa. The Namib Desert runs along its entire Atlantic Ocean coast. The inland area is a central plateau which reaches great heights in some places. The plateau is intermittently covered by grassland or forest. The Kalahari Desert is in the east. The average annual temperature on the coast is 62°F (16.7° C). The inland temperature averages at 70° F (21.1°C).

Eighty-five percent of the people are African, the majority of whom are Ovambo peoples. Others include the Herero, Kavango, Damara and San. The remainder are European or mixed African–European. The population is predominantly Christian. English is the official language, but Afrikaans is commonly used.

San hunter-gatherers inhabited Namibia by the first century B.C. The Nama people arrived in the sixth century A.D. During the seventeenth century, the Herero became established in the north. Early European explorers were repelled by the bleak coastal Namib Desert. Christian missionaries penetrated inland in the early nineteenth century.

Germany declared a protectorate over what it called South-West Africa in 1884. Tribal lands were seized. The Herero uprising of 1904 was ruthlessly suppressed and about 60,000 of the indigenous people were killed.

The German colony was seized by troops from the Union of South Africa in 1915. The League of Nations granted South Africa a mandate over it five years later. South Africa refused to acknowledge United Nations control of the territory after World War II. It ignored the United Nation's resolutions, dividing Namibia into ethnic homelands. Europeans controlled the diamond mines.

The South West African People's Organization (SWAPO) launched a guerrilla war against South Africa in 1966. South Africa introduced an apartheid-based constitution in 1977, despite United Nations recognition of SWAPO as the legitimate government. It blocked national elections because it feared SWAPO would win.

The United Nations supervised the elections of 1988. SWAPO leader Sam Nujoma was elected president. Namibia became independent on March 21, 1990. It adopted a new constitution and became a member of the Commonwealth of Nations. The constitution was changed in 1999, enabling Nujoma to win a third term. Namibia faced deteriorating health conditions, a wide econonic gap between classes and staggering unemployment at the outset of the 2000s.

GOVERNMENT
Website www.grnnet.gov.na
Capital Windhoek
Type of government Republic
Independence from South Africa (UN Trust Territory)
March 21, 1990
Voting Universal adult suffrage
Head of state President
Head of government President
Constitution 1990
Legislature
Bicameral Parliament
National Assembly (lower house),
National Council (upper house)
Judiciary High Court
Member of CN, IMF, OAU, UN, UNESCO, UNHCR, WHO, WTO

LAND AND PEOPLE
Land area 318,580 sq mi
(825,118 sq km)
Highest point Konigstein 8,505 ft
(2,606 m)
Coastline 976 mi (1,572 km)
Population 1,820,916
Major cities and populations
Winhoek 202,000
Ethnic groups
African 85%, European 7%, others
8%
Religions
Christianity 80%, traditional
animism 10%
Languages English (official),
Afrikaans, indigenous languages

ECONOMIC
Currency Namibian dollar
Industry
meat processing, seafood
processing, dairy, mining
Agriculture
millet, sorghum, nuts, livestock,
Natural resources
diamonds, copper, uranium, gold,
lead, tin, lithium, cadmium, zinc,
salt, vanadium, natural gas, seafood

Nauru

REPUBLIC OF NAURU

Nauru is in the central South Pacific Ocean just south of the equator. It is a raised oval-shaped coral island. Most of the people of Nauru live along a narrow, fertile coastal strip that encircles the island. The rest of the island consists of a central plateau that contains rich deposits of phosphate rock. The climate is tropical with high humidity and high temperatures all year round.

Most Nauruans are of Polynesian or mixed Micronesian–Melanesian backgrounds. Christianity is the primary religion. The Nauruan language is a mix of Polynesian, Micronesian and Melanesian dialects.

Little is known of the original Polynesian inhabitants. The crew of a British ship named it Pleasant Island in 1798. European traders arrived in the 1830s. It was annexed by Germany in 1888, under the pretext of ending indigenous clan warfare on the island. Britain began mining phosphate on the island in the late 1800s.

Australian troops occupied the island in 1914. A League of Nations mandate in 1920 placed the island under the administration of Australia, with Britain and New Zealand as co-trustees. The British Phosphate Commission was already exercising broad control over the country's mineral wealth.

The Japanese held the island during World War II. Nauru became a United Nations trust territory under Australian administration in 1947. Internal self-government was granted gradually from 1951 to 1966. Nauru gained its independence on January 31, 1968. Britain, Australia and New Zealand agreed to surrender mining interests to the Nauru Phosphate Corporation in 1970.

In 1989, Nauru sought compensation from Australia for environmental damage done by phosphate mining. The International Court of Justice ruled in Nauru's favor in 1992. Australia paid Nauru U.S. $66 million. New Zealand and Britain also paid nominal sums.

Nauru used its phosphate revenues for international investments. Poor management of these saw the island nation near bankruptcy by the late 1990s. Phosphate reserves are likely to run out by 2010.

The years since independence have brought several leaders to power, often after political upheavals occurred. An international task force threatened Nauru with sanctions in 2001 if its government failed to crack down on money laundering. Nauru accepted hundreds of Asian refugees on behalf of Australia in September of 2001, in return for increased aid.

Nepal

KINGDOM OF NEPAL

Located north of India, Nepal is famous as the home of Mount Everest, the world's tallest mountain. The Great Himalaya Mountains lie across the northern part of the country near China. The Valley of Kathmandu makes up much of the center of the country. A fertile region known as Terai, on the Ganges River, occupies the southern part of the country. Terai is sub-tropical, cool in winter, hot in summer. The Himalayas are alpine, with constant snow and sub-zero temperatures.

Sixty percent of the population is Nepalese. Hinduism is the state religion and there are significant numbers of Buddhists and Muslims. Nepali is the official language. Indigenous languages are also in use.

The Newar dynasty was established in central Nepal by the fourth century A.D. The Malla dynasty ruled from the tenth century. Rajput Gurkha warriors expanded Nepalese territory substantially and unified the nation, beginning in 1769. Gurkha King Prithvi Narayan Shah established a dynasty from which today's Nepalese royal family is descended.

China repelled Gurkha attempts to conquer Tibet in 1792. Gurkha advances into India prompted a war with Britain in 1814. Nepal lost the war and some of its territories.

The pro-British Rana family took control of the government in 1846, making the prime ministership hereditary. The role of monarch was to be a figurehead with nominal powers.

Political movements were established in the 1930s calling for democracy and an end to British influence. The Nepalese Congress Party (NCP) rebelled against the Rana regime in 1951. It was supported by King Tribhuvana. Several abrupt changes in government occurred during the next years, during which the king seized direct rule. King Tribhuvana was succeeded by his son Mahendra in 1955.

King Mahendra presented a new democratic constitution in 1958. Nepal's first elections were held the following year. The result was an overwhelming victory for the NCP and a new government was established. The king suspended the constitution and banned political parties in 1960. He adopted a new constitution. Birendra became king in 1972.

King Birendra permitted political parties and improved human rights after widespread demonstrations in 1990. A succession of unsuccessful coalition governments followed. Prince Dipendra, son of the king, killed his father and nine other members of the royal family before killing himself in 2001.

GOVERNMENT
Capital Kathmandu
Type of government
Constitutional monarchy
Voting Universal adult suffrage
Head of state Monarch
Head of government Prime Minister
Constitution 1990
Legislature
Bicameral Parliament
House of Representatives (lower house), National Council (upper house)
Judiciary Supreme Court
Member of
IMF, UN, UNESCO, WHO

LAND AND PEOPLE
Land area 54,362 sq mi (140,797 sq km)
Highest point Mount Everest 29,035 ft (8,850 m)
Population 25,284,463
Major cities and populations
Kathmandu 533,000
Lalitpur 190,000
Biratnagar 132,000
Ethnic groups Nepalese 60%, Bihari 19%, others 21%
Religions Hinduism 90%, Buddhism 5%, Islam 3%
Languages
Nepali (official), indigenous languages

ECONOMIC
Currency
Rupee
Industry
tourism, carpets, textiles, rice, jute, sugar milling, cement
Agriculture
rice, corn, wheat, sugar cane, root crops, dairy
Natural resources
quartz, timber, lignite, copper, cobalt, iron ore

Netherlands

KINGDOM OF THE NETHERLANDS

The Netherlands is the largest of the European nations referred to collectively as the Low Countries. The group, which includes Belgium and Luxembourg, is so named because of its location near or below sea level. The Netherlands is situated in northwestern Europe with a coastline on the North Sea. Most of the land is low-lying agricultural land. About a quarter of it lies below sea level. A complex system of man-made dikes minimizes the chance of flooding. The Waal, Maas, Issel, Rhine and Schelde rivers form a large delta before emptying into the North Sea. There are also canals which link with those of Germany and Belgium.

The Netherlands enjoys a temperate maritime climate. Winters are marked by cold winds sweeping across the landscape, while summers are warm and pleasant, particularly near the coast. Inland areas can be colder in winter and hotter in summer.

All but two percent of the people are Dutch. There are small communities of people from former Dutch colonies such as Suriname and Indonesia. While thirty-five percent of Dutch people claim no tie to any religion, the rest are almost all Christian. Dutch is the official language.

The Netherlands is particularly noted for its electrical and electronic equipment. Other major manufacturing includes textiles and clothing, processed food, plastics, refined petroleum, shipbuilding, iron and steel, transport equipment, chemicals and machinery. Natural resources are limited, the most common being natural gas and coal.

Farming is intensive. The Netherlands is well-known for its dairy products, particularly cheeses. Beet sugar and potatoes are the main crops grown and fresh flowers are also a significant export to all parts of the world.

Service industries are a key part of the Dutch economy. Rotterdam's port is one of the world's busiest, processing large volumes of European exports and imports through its vast and efficient facility. Amsterdam is also a major financial center for Europe. Tourism is highly developed with millions of visitors to the Netherlands from around the world. Amsterdam is one of Europe's most popular tourist destinations.

The head of state is the hereditary monarch, primarily a ceremonial position. The government is run by the prime minister and cabinet. The Dutch legislature, or States-General, consists of the First and Second Chambers. The 75 members of the First Chamber are elected by provincial legislatures. The 150 members of the

Netherlands

FLAT EARTH PICTURE GALLERY

Tulip growing is a major industry in the Netherlands — the flowers are exported around the world.

introduced their own culture to the area.

Germanic tribes moved across the land during the fourth century A.D. It was incorporated into the Frankish Empire and Christianity became widespread in the seventh century. The decline of the Franks coincided with the arrival of the Vikings, who established a feudal system. The eastern region was incorporated into the Holy Roman Empire.

The region was known for its active trade from many different ports. The ongoing battle against North Sea flooding resulted in reclamation of large areas. This new coastal land, being free of the feudal system, created a class of independent peasants.

The French Dukes of Burgundy replaced existing nobility in the fourteenth century. The marriage of Mary of Burgundy to the Habsburg Maximilian brought the Netherlands, Belgium and Luxembourg into Austrian Habsburg control in 1477.

The Habsburg and Spanish royal families were joined following the coronation of Charles V in 1511. The Low Countries became a Spanish province in 1555. They were ruled by the unpopular tyrant King Philip II.

Second Chamber are elected by a popular vote on a proportional representation system. Members of both chambers have terms of up to four years.

Historical accounts of the Netherlands date from the first century B.C. when Roman forces conquered most of the present area of the country. The region was inhabited by Frisians, a German tribe which lived in the north. Peace and prosperity prevailed. The Romans constructed temples, established large farms and

Calvinism, a Protestant movement, had made serious advances in the previously Catholic empire. Philip attempted to reinforce Catholicism by introducing the Spanish Inquisition to the Netherlands. This provoked a revolt led by William the Silent of Orange. The Spanish army was expelled in 1574.

The non-Catholic northern Low Countries provinces declared independence from Spain in 1576, becoming the Dutch Republic of the United Provinces of the Netherlands. The Catholic southern provinces, roughly the area of present-day Belgium and Luxembourg, remained loyal to Spain.

The new Dutch republic became embroiled in the Catholic–Protestant Thirty Years War from 1618 to 1648. The Peace of Westphalia in 1648 finally confirmed the legitimacy of the Netherlands. Large numbers of Protestants fled the southern Low Countries provinces to the Netherlands.

The Dutch built a powerful trading empire during the ensuing peace. The Dutch East India Company, formed in 1602, secured dominion over the Spice Islands, now Indonesia. It developed a lucrative trade in spices much in demand throughout Europe. The Dutch West India Company, established in 1621, took on a similar role in the Caribbean. These private companies colonized various parts of the world with support from the Netherlands government.

Much of the prosperity of the Netherlands was generated by the many refugees it admitted. Jews from Spain and Portugal made substantial contributions to business. Persecuted Huguenots poured into the country from France. Commercial success brought artistic success. Painters such as Vermeer and Rembrandt reached their creative peaks at this time.

The Netherlands competed fiercely with Britain. They clashed regularly over colonial holdings and trading rights. The Dutch North American colony of New Amsterdam was lost to Britain in 1666. The Netherlands' control of the colony of Suriname in Central America was confirmed in the 1667 Treaty of Breda.

France invaded the Netherlands in 1672. Jan de Witt, head of state, was murdered. William III of Orange became head of state, or stadtholder. Relations with Britain improved when William and his wife, Mary II, became joint rulers of Britain in 1689. Further clashes with France came during the War of the Grand Alliance (1688–97) and the War of the Spanish Succession (1701–14).

William IV of Orange became hereditary head of state in 1747. His successor William V, facing mounting

Enjoying the outdoor café life in The Hague.

Netherlands

BRAND X PICTURES

calls for reform, called on Prussian troops to maintain order in 1787.

The French Revolution inspired Dutch dissidents, who aided a French conquest of the Netherlands in 1794. William V fled to Britain and the Netherlands became the Batavian Republic the following year. It was converted into a kingdom for Napoleon Bonaparte's brother, Louis, in 1806. It became a French province four years later. The British seized Dutch colonial possessions, including the Cape Colony in southern Africa, Ceylon (Sri Lanka) and half of Guyana, during this time. The East Indies (Indonesia) and other Caribbean holdings were later restored to the Netherlands.

The independence of the Netherlands was restored in 1815 by the Congress of Vienna, after the fall of Napoleon. The area of present-day Belgium and Luxembourg was made part of the Netherlands. William V's son, known as King William I, was monarch.

William's authoritarianism alienated the southern Catholic population imbued with the principles of the French Revolution. Belgium and Luxembourg declared themselves independent in 1830. The Dutch recognized the separation in 1839.

Windmills, such as these at Kinderdijk, are symbolic of Dutch industry of the past.

King William II oversaw considerable social and economic reform after his father's forced abdication in 1840. The Dutch embraced the Industrial Revolution enthusiastically after 1860. Developments were funded by vast profits made in the East Indies and other colonies. The colonial peoples suffered appalling social and labor conditions while the homeland flourished.

William III died in 1890, leaving his wife to rule as

regent until their daughter Wilhelmina came of age eight years later. Wilhelmina ruled for the next fifty years. The Netherlands' sponsorship of a peace conference in 1907 resulted in the establishment of the International Court of Justice at The Hague.

The Netherlands remained neutral during World War I. It suffered economic hardship due to the Allied blockade of the European continent. The prosperity of the 1920s was replaced by economic turmoil during the Depression. Proportional representation voting led to a large number of political parties in the parliament creating highly unstable government coalitions.

Germany overran the country and destroyed much of the great port at Rotterdam in May of 1940. Queen Wilhelmina and her ministers formed a government-in-exile in Britain. Harassment by Dutch resistance groups provoked brutal German reprisals. Ninety percent of the 112,000 Dutch Jews were executed in German concentration camps. The people of the Dutch East Indies suffered under Japanese occupation.

The years following World War II were marked by intensive efforts to rebuild the country and to restore its trade and industry. The Netherlands became a founding member of the United Nations in 1945. Two years later it joined Belgium and Luxembourg in the BENELUX Economic Union. The Netherlands joined the North Atlantic Treaty Organization in 1949, the European Defense Community Treaty in 1952 and the London-Paris accords in 1955, making it a full-fledged member of the Western European multinational defense establishment. The nation was at the forefront of planning that eventually led to the creation of the European Union.

Independence leaders in the East Indies declared a Republic of Indonesia in 1945. This was firmly resisted by the Nether-

Amsterdam is renowned for its extensive network of canals.

Netherlands

lands government despite support for the Indonesians around the world. The image of the Dutch colonizers as harsh masters did not aid their cause. The government bowed to the inevitable and granted Indonesia independence in 1949.

Queen Wilhelmina abdicated in 1948 in favor of her daughter Juliana. Juliana's daughter, Beatrix, gave birth to a son in 1967, the first male in the Dutch succession since 1884. Beatrix succeeded to the throne in 1980.

The Netherlands enjoyed considerable economic prosperity from the 1950s. Vast land reclamation projects greatly increased the area in coastal regions and helped with reinforcement of flood defenses.

The late 1940s and 1950s were dominated by Labor party government. The Roman Catholic People's party came to power in 1959 and retained influenced throughout the 1960s. Power has shifted among a number of vastly different coalitions since that time.

Netherlands Guyana, renamed Suriname, became independent in 1975. Hundreds of thousands of its people immigrated to the Netherlands, placing a huge burden on the Dutch economy.

Riots against the government in the Netherlands Antilles required Dutch troops to assist police in 1969. The Netherlands Antilles remains a Dutch territory. Aruba opted for autonomous status within the Netherlands in 1986.

Dutch governments have implemented some of the world's most liberal social policies in recent years. Prostitution has been legalized. Laws against the sale of drugs such as marijuana are not enforced. Euthanasia under specified conditions was legalized, making the Netherlands the first country to sanction doctor-assisted suicides. Same-sex domestic partnerships have been recognized since 1998. The lower house of the parliament voted to extend full legal sanction to same-sex marriages in 2000.

The peaceful political scene was shattered by the murder of right-wing politician Pim Fortuyn in May of 2002. It was initially assumed that the killing was a result of Fortuyn's controversial opinions on immigration and refugees. It was later determined that the murder was motivated by opposition to Fortuyn's environmental policies. The Dutch people voted strongly for the right-wing candidates of the Christian Democrat Party shortly after Fortuyn's murder.

NETHERLANDS OVERSEAS TERRITORIES

Aruba

Aruba is an island off the northern coast of Venezuela, in the southern Caribbean Sea. It was home to Arawak Indians until the seventeenth century. The Dutch claimed it in 1634, but no real development occurred until an oil refinery was established in 1929. It was grouped with the other Netherlands Antilles islands in 1954. The people of Aruba were never content with this arrangement. The island became a separate autonomous Dutch territory on January 1, 1986. The International Monetary Fund commended Aruba in 2001 for improved controls on its off-shore banking enterprises.

Netherlands Antilles

This territory is made up of the islands of Curaçao, Bonaire, St. Martin, Saba and St. Eustasius in the Caribbean Sea. The original inhabitants were Arawaks and Caribs. Spanish settlers arrived on Curaçao in 1511. The islands were captured in 1634 by the Netherlands, which quickly developed them as a slave trading center for the region. Internal self-government was granted in 1954. Referendums held in the 1990s all resulted in strong votes to remain part of the Netherlands.

New Zealand

GOVERNMENT

Website www.govt.nz
Capital Wellington
Type of government
Parliamentary democarcy
Independence from Britain
September 26, 1907 (dominion status)
Voting Universal adult suffrage
Head of state
British Crown,
represented by Governor-General
Head of government Prime Minister
Constitution 1907
Legislature Unicameral Parliament
Judiciary High Court
Member of APEC, CN, IMF, OECD, SPF, UN, UNESCO, WHO, WTO

LAND AND PEOPLE

Land area 104,453 sq mi
(270,534 sq km)
Highest point Mount Cook
12,349 ft (3,764 m)
Coastline 9,403 mi (15,134 km)
Population 3,864,129
Major cities and populations
Auckland 1.1 million
Wellington 350,000
Christchurch 340,000
Ethnic groups European 80%,
Maori 13%, Polynesian 5%
Religions Christianity
Languages
English, Maori (both official)

ECONOMIC

Currency New Zealand dollar
Industry
food processing, wood products,
paper products, textiles, agricultural
products, tourism, mining, wines
Agriculture
wheat, barley, potatoes, fruits,
vegetables, wool, beef, dairy,
seafood
Natural resources
natural gas, iron ore, sand, coal,
timber, gold, limestone

New Zealand is located in the South Pacific Ocean southeast of Australia. It is comprised of two large islands, North Island and South Island and numerous smaller islands. The North Island is known for its geysers, hot springs and active volcanoes. The South Island is dominated by the Southern Alps and a coastline indented with deep fjords. The climate is temperate and rainfall is plentiful. The northern regions can be sub-tropical at times. The far south experiences extreme cold.

New Zealanders are primarily of European descent. The indigenous Maori people make up thirteen percent of the total population. Five percent are from Pacific Island backgrounds. The remainder are Asian minorities. Christianity accounts for about two-thirds of the people. While English is the official language, Maori is widely used.

New Zealand was first settled in A.D. 800 by Polynesian migrants. Their civilization gradually developed into the unique Maori culture. The Dutch were the first Europeans on New Zealand's shores. Explorer Abel Tasman sighted the South Island in 1642, naming it Staaten Landt. It later became Nieew Zeeland.

Captain James Cook charted the coast in 1769. Three years later a French expedition, led by Marion du Fresne, clashed with Maori in a battle which killed 250 people. Whalers and sealers were making regular calls within twenty years. Christian missionaries had some success after 1814.

British settlers began arriving by the 1830s. The resultant clashes with the Maori forced Britain to make New Zealand a colony. Lieutenant-Governor William Hobson signed the Treaty of Waitangi with fifty Maori chieftains on February 6, 1840. The chieftains retained ownership of the land which the British could purchase. Sovereignty was ceded to Britain.

New Zealand was granted internal self-government in

A typical New Zealand rural scene.

FLAT EARTH PICTURE GALLERY

New Zealand

FLAT EARTH PICTURE GALLERY

The spectacular Franz Josef Glacier on the South Island.

1852. Agreeable climate and good grazing land made New Zealand highly popular with British settlers. It had also avoided the stigma of convict settlement which tainted the Australian colonies. Disputes over land ownership erupted into battles in the Taranaki region in 1860. Troops were brought from Australia to aid local forces.

The discovery of gold in 1865 brought even more settlers to the colony. Gold mining and sheep raising soon became its major industries. The introduction of refrigerated shipping in the 1880s enabled lamb and mutton to be exported to Britain. This further stimulated settlement.

The 1890s was a golden era of social progress for New Zealand. It led the world in the labor arbitration, workplace safety and industrial relations. It was the first country in the world to grant women the vote in 1893.

Proposals for a union of New Zealand and Australia in a federation of British colonies led to nothing. New Zealand became a self-governing dominion of the British Empire in 1907.

New Zealand fought for the Allied forces in World War I. About 16,000 of its men were killed and another 40,000 were wounded in the fighting.

New Zealand once more led the world in progressive social policies from the 1930s. Free medical treatment was introduced in 1938. New Zealand troops once again joined the Allies in World War II, fighting in Greece, Cyprus, North Africa, Italy and the Pacific.

New Zealand loosened its political ties with Britain after the war. New Zealand's agricultural industry, however, still relied heavily on Britain as its primary market. British membership in the European Economic Community dealt a devastating blow to the export earnings of New Zealand in the 1970s.

The last half of the twentieth century saw frequent shifts in leadership between the Labour and National parties. Economic issues, specifically those involving industry, most often brought changes in leadership.

Labour party leader David Lange was elected prime minister in 1984. He restructured the economy through privatization of industry. The country adopted an anti-nuclear defense policy. The United States suspended its security agreement with New Zealand after the nation banned nuclear vessels from its ports in the mid-1980s.

Prime Minister Helen Clark softened some of the harsh economic policies following Labour's reelection in 1999. State ownership of key infrastructure was again proposed. Maori demands for social and economic rights continue to be a major focus.

Nicaragua

REPUBLIC OF NICARAGUA

Nicaragua is the largest republic in Central America. The Nicaragua Highlands cross the country from northwest to southeast. Several mountain ranges, including the Cordillera Isabelia, cut the highlands from east to west. A great basin on the west includes two large lakes, Nicaragua and Managua. A chain of volcanoes rises between these lakes and the Pacific coast. The marshy and inhospitable Caribbean region is known as the Mosquito Coast. The climate is tropical with a wet season from May to January.

Seventy percent of the people are mestizos, a mix of Spanish and indigenous backgrounds. About fifteen percent are European, while the remainder are either indigenous people or descendants of African slaves. Nicaragua is overwhelmingly Christian. Its official language is Spanish.

Very few records of early Nicaraguan society exist. The Lenca people had developed a civilization after many years of settlement. Christopher Columbus sighted the area in 1502. A Spanish expedition in 1522 crushed native resistance and settlements were founded.

Nicaragua declared itself independent of Spanish control in 1821. For two years it was part of the Mexican Empire before joining the United Provinces of Central America from 1823 until 1838.

Britain established an enclave at San Juan del Norte on the Mosquito Coast in 1848. Tensions erupted between Britain and the United States over the proposal for a canal through Nicaragua, linking the Caribbean and Pacific.

Politics was a constant battle between the Liberals, based in León, and the Conservatives, based in Granada. A new capital city was established at Managua in 1855. That year William Walker, an American, led a gang of mercenaries to depose the Conservative government. He declared himself president but was forced to step down in 1857.

The Liberals took power in 1893 under President José Santos Zelaya. He remained in office for 16 years, ruling as a dictator. Zelaya was forced out of office as Adolfo Diaz was elected provisional president. Diaz asked the U. S. for assistance following a revolt against his government in 1912. U.S. Marines restored peace.

The subsequent Bryan–Cahmorro Treaty gave the United States exclusive rights to construct a canal through the country which would connect the Caribbean Sea and the Pacific Ocean. Guerrillas fought a running battle with the U.S. forces for many years. The marines withdrew in 1925, returned the following year after a coup attempt and finally departed seven years later.

Nicaragua

General Anastasio Somoza was president from 1937 until his assassination in 1956. Corruption reached staggering levels under his leadership. The Somoza family controlled the nation for another twenty years after his death. Nicaragua fought beside the Allied powers in World War II. It became a charter member of the United Nations in 1945.

An earthquake destroyed Managua in 1972, klling 5,000 and injuring 20,000. The Somozas declared martial law. The government was subsequently accused of widespread human rights abuses. The opposition Sandanista National Liberation Front, formed in 1962, deposed the Somoza regime in 1979.

Political and social reform followed quickly. Many key industries and utilities were nationalized and land reform instituted. The United States severed economic aid in 1981 and promoted an opposition Contra guerrilla movement.

The Sandanistas held their first election in 1984. Their leader Daniel Ortega Saavedra was elected president. Aid poured in from the Soviet Union, but the economic cost of the war against the Contras was debilitating. Protests against severe austerity measures prompted Ortega to declare a state of emergency.

Violeta Barrios de Chamorro won the elections of 1990. The United States dropped its economic sanctions and resumed large-scale aid. A cease-fire agreement was reached with the Contras.

A huge hurricane swept the country in 1998, killing 4,000 people and devastating the economy. Aid from the United States and Europe has helped with recovery from the destruction caused by the Contra movement's activities.

Nicaraguan boys pose in front of a mural celebrating the Sandanistas.